Endorsemen

I believe the generational blessing
being poured out on this cursed land ᴀᴏ ᴀᴇᴏᴀᴏᴀᴇ ᴀᴀᴇ ᴀᴇᴀᴀᴀ
of the fathers to the children, and the children to the
fathers to stop the curse and restore His blessings.

Bruce Brodowski, in his experience of a Baptism of Love
and the Spirit of Sonship, is a sign that the author can
say, "Abba". *My Father My Son* is not just a book to be
read, but a life to be experienced. Read it, then let it read
you. You will never be the same.

Leif Hetland, President,
Global Mission Awareness

As you read this book, prepare to have a life-changing
encounter with the heart of God.

Grant Mullen MC
Author of *Emotionally Free*

So many people I meet have an issue with God the Father
because their relationship with their earthly father has
been missing or strained. Brodowski sheds light on the little
boy and the man who lost so much yet gained everything.
This book is well worth reading about the healing of a soul.

The Rev. Nigel Mumford, Director
The Oratory of Christ the Healer, Christ the King
Spiritual Life Center
Greenwich, NY

A well needed and well timed book for all those who need
to discover the healing of their orphaned hearts and come
home to the Father heart of God.

Reverend Russ Parker, Director
Acorn Christian Healing Foundation, UK

My Father

My Son

Also by Bruce Brodowski
The Dad I Never Knew:
A War Orphan's Search for Inner Healing

My Father My Son

Healing the Orphan Heart
With the Father's Love

BRUCE BRODOWSKI

Carolinas
Ecumenical
Healing
Ministries

Scripture quotations taken from the New American Standard
Bible® Copyright © 1960, 1962, 1963, 1968, 1971, 1972,
1973, 1975, 1977, 1995 by The Lockman Foundation. Used by
permission (www.Lockman.org).

Copyright © Judy Landt 2008, sermon used by permission.

Copyright permission to quote "From Orphan to Heirs" by Mark
Stibbe has been obtained from BRF, 15 The Chambers, Vineyard,
Abingdon, OX14 3FE, UK.

Materials from "Agape Road" by Bob Mumford, copyright 2006;
"Experiencing Father's Embrace" by Jack Frost, copyright 2006; and
"Spiritual Slavery to Spiritual Sonship" by Jack Frost, copyright
2006, used by permission of Destiny Image Publishers, 167 Walnut
Bottom Road, Shippensburg, PA (www.DestinyImage.com).

Book and cover design by Five Rainbows Services,
www.FiveRainbows.com

Cover painting : ALG188735
Credit: "God the Father Blessing" (oil on panel) by Raphael,
Galleria Nazionale dell'Umbria, Perugia, Italy/ Alinari/ The
Bridgeman Art Library Nationality / copyright status: Italian
/ out of copyright. Used with copyright permission from The
Bridgeman Art Library, 65 East 93rd St, New York, NY,

ISBN: 978-0-9826581-1-6

Carolinas Ecumenical Healing Ministries
Matthews, NC 28105
www.AngelFire.com/nc3/chm

Carolinas Ecumenical Healing Ministries

Permission by
Statesville Stained Glass

www.CEHM.info

A large portion of the proceeds from the sale of this book will go to support the continuing ministry work of Carolinas Ecumenical Healing Ministries. We thank you for helping us bring the healing ministry of Jesus Christ to the world. May God bless you abundantly.

Contents

Acknowledgments

I humbly thank the Father for encouraging me to go forward with the writing of this book and providing the inspired words when needed. I thank Him for opening doors that allowed contacting people for copyright permissions, chapter contributions, manuscript reviews, and expert advice.

I thank Russ Parker for his support through the process of this book and for encouraging me to go forward when I had no intentions to write another book, especially this one.

I thank Randy Clark and Global Awakening for their ministry and conferences where I first encountered the teaching on the orphan heart. It was here that opened my eyes to the need for an all-encompassing book on the subject. Global Awakening has changed my life and my ministry.

I thank Leif Hetland for graciously taking the time from his very busy ministry schedule to review the manuscript and submit his endorsement. If Leif hadn't prayed over me in Fredericksburg, Virginia, to break the orphan spirit, I would have not been drawn towards learning more about this part of inner healing ministry.

I thank Trisha Frost and Shiloh Place Ministries for teaching about Experiencing Father's Embrace in their ministry schools and the extensive amount of coverage on the Orphan Heart.

I thank Rodney Hogue for contributing to a chapter on the importance of forgiveness.

I thank Harold Martin, which became an important part of my life in inner healing, for his contributions to the book and for the information on healing the orphan heart. I thank Dr. Grant Mullen for taking the time to review the book and graciously submit his endorsement.

Finally, I thank my wife, Ellen, for her love, kindness, and patience throughout the months of research, rewrites, editing, and publishing of *My Father, My Son*.

Foreword

We are in a major pandemic of fatherlessness. This is not caused just by the absence of a father figure in the home, but also by the son's inability or hindrance to receive fathering. Hurt people hurt people—wounded people wound people. Fathers cannot be the fathers they need to be because they have never been sons. Sons cannot be the sons they need to be because they have been wounded by their fathers. So now we have this epidemic of fatherlessness created by orphans—natural and emotional—begetting and raising orphans rather than sons begetting and raising sons. The number one contributor to fatherlessness is the "Orphan Heart." Both the natural orphan and the emotional orphan develop the orphan heart as they take on orphan mentality, and develop orphan thinking as a result of the wounding they have received and the lies they have believed. This is why it is so important for you, the people in the church today, to recognize what the devil is doing in your life. We need to recognize how far out of our position of sonship we are living; to recognize how deep orphan mentality has become ingrained in our life; and to realize how much we are living out of an orphan heart rather than the heart of a son/daughter.

One of the greatest obstacles and biggest strongholds that we need to overcome to be able to move into the reality of our sonship is the pandemic of orphan mentality that has consumed the church and our society of believers. We were created in the image and likeness of God for communion, fellowship, and intimacy with Him. Because of all the Father has accomplished by the blood of Jesus, the devil, and all the hordes of hell, *cannot* stop us from moving into our as created positions of sons and daughters. So, just like in the garden, he uses the deception of orphan thinking, the subtle impartation of the orphan heart to rob us of what belongs to us. The heart of sonship belongs to you. An orphan heart is something that developed within you as a result of the wounding you received and the lies you believed. We need to recognize the reality of both and understand why we are where we are. We need to begin to move progressively and purposely towards our position of sonship.

From the very conception of mankind in the heart of the Father God, we were created to be sons and daughters. (For clarification, when we speak of sons, we mean both sons and daughters) We were created on purpose, with a purpose, and for a purpose: God is love (1 John 4:16). We were created by love, for love, and to love. We were created for sonship, created as objects of the Father's affections. We were created to be vessels of his love, to receive His love, and give it away to the world around us.

The sad reality is that this is very foreign to most Christians today. Most believers struggle with both giving and receiving love. They struggle with purpose, struggle with having a destiny, and above all struggle with sonship. If the basic concepts of sonship are foundational to our existence, why is there such a struggle for us to be what we were created to be? What happened to the process?

We all need to understand that there is no such thing as private sin. The sin of Adam and Eve did not affect just them. Their sin became generational. Their sin imparted a sin nature, or the natural tendency towards sin, into all following generations. We are the seed from their seed. Their sin ultimately required the blood of the Son of God to bring about justification and forgiveness.

Sin separated the Father from His son. It caused a breach in fellowship and loss of intimacy. Through sin and disobedience, not only did man receive the impartation of a sin nature from Satan's deception, but he also received the impartation of Satan's orphan heart/orphan mentality. From that point forward orphan mentality became a generational issue. We are all born with a tendency to move into orphan mentality, rather than live in sonship. Now instead of all creation being in tune with man, the creation waits in eager expectation for the sons of God to be revealed.

I first met Bruce Brodowski in April 2009 at Shiloh Place Ministries where I was teaching on Embracing Father's Love. At that time he was struggling with receiving the Father's Love. He was also deeply into research for his manuscript *My Father, My Son*. I realized that we both shared a heart's desire to see the natural and emotional orphans set free from the debilitating bondage they are currently living in.

There is a way back to the Father's heart through the inner healing that comes from recognizing the wounding we have suffered and removing the lies we have believed. I feel that "My Father, My Son, Healing the Orphan Heart with the Father's Love" provides any reader with what they need to make this journey. This book not only identifies the symptoms of the orphan heart, but also lays out the path to wholeness through a greater understanding of the Father's intense love for us. It is only through a supernatural encounter with the Father's love that the wounding can be healed and the lies banished forever. This book by Bruce Brodowski will facilitate that process.

Pastor Harold Martin
Lake Marion Christian Fellowship
Santee, SC

Preface

In 2008, after coming home from Guatemala, I felt a force driving me to complete a writing project I was working on. I was doing research about my dad for my book *The Dad I Never Knew, A War Orphan's Search for Inner Healing*. He was killed in Germany in World War II. I considered the number of fatherless orphans from both World War I and II from all countries. I contemplated what affect being fatherless had on the child development of these war orphans and how this may have affected the spiritual culture of the world. I decided also to include those children with physically present fathers that were emotionally absent. As a healing prayer minister, I realized that there was an enormous need for healing ministry for this large segment of society.

While I was attending a Randy Clark Global Awakening Conference, speaker Leif Hetland was teaching on a Friday night on the orphan heart. I was having a hard time receiving the Father's love. I realized Leif was describing me. Therefore, I later went up for prayer and made sure that Leif prayed over me. The next thing I remember was checking out the ceiling while lying on the floor. This was unique for me, because over a period

of eight years, I may have rested in the spirit four times.
I just don't slam dunk often. I felt that I had had an experiential encounter that brought me closer to the Father. I
had always had a close, intimate relationship with Jesus,
but for me the Father was not approachable.

From the teaching on orphan heart, I hypothesized that
all fatherless orphans experience the same emotional childhood developmental problems that need to be addressed
in healing ministry. In my research I found information
about those emotional characteristics in the writings of
Mark Stibbe, Leif Hetland, Jack Frost, Jack Winter, Donna
J. Kazenske, Judith MacNutt , Dennis and Matthew Linn,
James Jordan, Robert Holmes, Pastor Harold Martin, and
Pastor Dave Toyne; and in other source materials. There
was a common theme that some orphans may experience
the following: "Inability to have lasting relationships, a
hatred of authority, a general distrust for leaders, a general lack of direction in their life, and an inability to make
key, strategic decisions. Drawing near, and then backing
away from intimacy. A sense that people are just going
to reject them anyway. A gnawing sense of failure, never
quite good enough. An inexplicable drive to succeed, to
win, and prove themselves."[1] They are constantly seeking
the affirmation that they are lovable and capable of being
loved. Their daddy wasn't around to tell them that.

As I reviewed these characteristics of the orphan spirit,
I found myself checking off mentally the ones that fit my
personal situation, which were the majority of them. Then
I assumed that all orphans have an orphan spirit and need
healing ministry. The logic was obvious to me. These are
the characteristics of an orphan spirit. All orphans have
an orphan spirit. We develop an orphan spirit because we
are orphans. Therefore, all orphans have these characteristics. However, the assumptions fell apart when I tried to
obtain testimonials from orphans to support my supposition.

One woman emailed me and said, "You might want to look at your assumptions for your conclusions about this particular group of orphans, as well as your own objectivity, before proceeding much further. You cannot assume that every war orphan has your issues. I have found, knowing many among us very well, that among us all, each has his/her own issues, and I do, too. Some of us have worked through them in one way or another, and some have been more damaged than others have. We are a variable lot and cannot be painted with a broad brush. Most have none of the characteristics that you initially described."

I realized that these are mental attitudes and not personal characteristics. Right away, I was asking myself: what are these characteristics based on, and how were they determined to be correct? Not all orphans would have the same mental attitude.

Trisha Frost of Shiloh Place Ministries has stated, "We have based our teachings on our personal experience with those we have ministered to in our encounters where we share on orphan heart issues."

In October 2008, I attended a Healing Winds Conference at Lake Logan, NC. At that time I reviewed my finished work, *The Dad I Never Knew,* with some friends. I talked about my theory of a paradigm shift in the spiritual culture because of World War II. Reverend Russ Parker said to me with a smile, "I believe you are on to something, mate." I said, "Russ, how much information is out there on the orphan heart subject?" He answered, "Not much, let me know what you come up with, mate, and I will review it." Thus, this was the start of *My Father, My Son: Healing the Orphan Heart with the Father's Love.*

If a child has a father physically present BUT emotionally absent, never AFFIRMING to that child that he is well pleased with his child, the child is emotionally an orphan with an orphan heart condition.

Even if a fatherless child has a loving extended family for support as I did, the child requires biologically, emotionally, psychologically, spiritually, and as part of the child's DNA, an EXPERIENCE of his father's love and affirmation. Without this love and affirmation, the child in most cases grows into adulthood with possible emotional and developmental problems. This book is about inner healing, healing an orphan heart.

Introduction

I believe what I have written is of importance to all people and all ministries. Today, more children than ever are in fatherless homes. Those who have biological fathers physically present are often without fathers emotionally. This is true not only in the United States, but throughout the world. Millions of children do not have a place of security, protection, comfort, and identity. They do not have a place where they receive a purpose in their lives. They do not have a place where they receive encouragement and affirmation. Many join gangs to fill the affirmation void in their lives.

Dr. Mark Stibbe is founder and leader of the Father's House Trust in the UK, a charity dedicated to taking the Father's love to the fatherless all over the world. Mark has recently stated at a conference:

> Today, there is a major pandemic sweeping across the earth. It is a pandemic of fatherlessness. More than at any other time in history, fatherhood is under attack and the consequences socially have become devastating. That is the bad news. The good news is that the church

has the antidote! It is the wonderful love of Abba Father revealed by Jesus and made available for all through the past event of the Cross and the continuing work of the Spirit. In this strategic season there is a call from heaven for the church to enter into the fullness of the Father's love, so that we can then be channels of this "love of all loves" to the fatherless throughout the world.[2]

I believe that millions of orphans in this world need healing of an orphan heart and that the importance of doing so is now becoming known to healing ministries. Wounded people wound people. Hurt people hurt people. What we feel to be true is true to us, even if it is a lie. My hope is that this book will reveal healing of an orphan heart to people throughout the world and help accomplish an awakening to do just that. The sins of the fathers, father issues, and mother issues are flowing down the river into the pool of future generations.

I discovered that much of the information available on healing the orphan heart is scattered and difficult to locate. In addition, I realized that the information is not gathered in one single source. This, therefore, is a compilation of material from many sources into a single reference book that explains what an orphan heart/orphan spirit is, discusses its history—how it developed into a paradigm shift in the emotional, political, and spiritual culture of post-World War II and subsequent generations —and reveals how those who need healing can go about seeking inner healing for the wounds an orphan heart created in their souls

History has recorded events of World War I, the Spanish Civil War, World War II, and one hundred additional conflicts in the second half of the twentieth century. These events include inhumane horrors and unthinkable massacres, all for the idealisms of a few. Never in the history of humanity has so much destruction been experienced nor should it ever be unleashed again. Who could have ever imagined Hitler's extermination of Jews in concentration camps or the instant vaporization of Japanese by atomic bombs at Hiroshima and Nagasaki?

> It is a fact that Hitler devoted his life to the occult and the study of the art of Black Magic. Hitler redefined the concept that death of the right people, like the Jew, could be beneficial; even more than beneficial, such death could result in the "healing" of the nation. His genocidal "Final Solution" became the obvious necessary step through the shedding of blood to achieving this "healing" of the German body. Hitler considered Christianity to be weak, beggarly and Pauline Jewish! Therefore, he stated his objective to be to "tearing up Christianity root and branch." As soon as he was finished totally annihilating the Jews, Hitler planned to turn on Christianity with the same Hellish fervor.[3]

Little did the men and women who fought in World War II realize that they were engaged in a spiritual conflict.

I am an American World War II orphan child born without a father in June of 1945. The dictionary defines "orphan" as "a child that has lost both parents," however here it is used to refer to fathers only. When referring to war orphans, this would indicate the loss of the father or "fatherless child." According to the Department of Veterans Affairs, there are 183,000 of us fatherless children. Although the precise numbers of World War II deaths are impossible to determine, these represent but a fraction of the total number of deaths that occurred. The countries involved in WWII were USSR, China, Germany, Poland, Japan, Yugoslavia, Rumania, France, Hungary, Austria, Greece, United States, Italy, Czechoslovakia, Great

Britain, The Netherlands, Belgium, Finland, Canada, India, Australia, Albania, Spain, Bulgaria, New Zealand, Norway, South Africa, Luxembourg, and Denmark. The total death count for both military personnel and civilians was approximately 56,150,000. Millions more were slaughtered in the trench warfare of World War I.

Therefore, the number of fatherless war children is astounding. Many of them have felt characteristics of an orphan heart, which encompasses a deep, dark, empty hole of missing pieces in their lives. For them, this was the consequence of war. World War II caused a paradigm shift in the emotional, political, and spiritual culture of the world. This was due to the void of a father's influence and love in the home. Millions of children now grew up without fathers. In addition, some governments adopted postwar policies that forcefully separated illegitimate children of enemy or occupying soldiers from their native mothers, and evacuated them to other countries to insure the purity of the future generations of that country, aiding in the devil's work.

The father of lies will do anything he can to break up the love and security in the home. The lack of a father's affirmation during childhood development created generations of orphan heart children that had a profound powerful affect on the future. The political and psychological policies justifying the separation of children from their mothers also caused storge deprivation symptoms, opening the door for the deterioration of religion and belief in God to the point of what it is today. Moral degradation became part of the fabric of the social culture. It evolved during the 1960s, an era that denotes the complex of interrelated cultural and political trends which occurred roughly during the years 1956 to 1974 in the West. The United States, Great Britain, France, Canada, Australia, Spain, Italy, and West Germany, in particular, experienced social and political upheaval, but it was not limited to these countries, and included such nations as Japan, Mexico, and others. This resulted from the post-World War II generation looking for love and affirmation. Its members wanted to know that they were loved, lovable, and belonged somewhere.

> In the United States, the Sixties as they are known in popular culture today lasted from about 1963 to 1971. The term is used descriptively by historians, journalists, and other objective academics; nostalgically by those who participated in the counter-culture and social revolution; and pejoratively by those who perceive the era as one of irresponsible excess and flamboyance. The decade was also labeled the Swinging Sixties because of the libertine attitudes that emerged during this decade. Rampant drug use has become inextricably associated with the counter-culture of the era, as Jefferson Airplane co-founder Paul Kantner mentions: "If you can remember anything about the sixties, you weren't really there."[4]

In a newspaper article mental health professional John Rosemond stated:

> In the 1960s, American parents stopped going to their elders for advice and began going instead to mental health professionals. So we created a philosophy that was 180 degrees removed from the philosophy that had successfully guided every previous generation of parents. The centerpiece of this new point of view was the notion that high self esteem is a good thing and that parents should make sure their children acquire it. Mind you, we made this up. Absolutely no empirical evidence, obtained by scientific means, existed to support this claim. It just sounded good.[5]

Notice that self esteem and not God or God's love was emphasized. Rosemond finishes with this statement:

> The self esteem movement has damaged children, families, schools, and culture. I propose that we begin the invigorating, rejuvenating process of finding our way back home.[6]

In addition, every fatherless child, whether male or female, may encounter the same orphan spirit and orphan heart. The number of fatherless homes continues to increase from generation to generation. A child can also feel fatherless even if a father is present. Those that have biological fathers physically present can be without a father emotionally. Not only is this true in the United States, but it is also occurring throughout the world. Millions of children today are feeling that they do not have a place of security, protection, comfort, and identity; that they do not have a place where they receive a purpose and destiny in their lives; and that they do not have a place where they receive encouragement and affirmation. They are now joining gangs to fill the void in their lives. They are craving the love and affirmation they did not receive from their parents. Some even look to fill that emotional depravation in a homosexual life style. What they need is to experience the love of the Father.

War Children

The war children of World War II are now in their sixties. According to Emmy E. Werner in her book, *Through the Eyes of Innocent*, there are only a handful of studies that follow children of World War II into adulthood. She states that these studies and her interviews with a dozen childhood survivors tell a similar story.

> Across the boundaries of time and place, the children of World War II have grown into adults with an extraordinary affirmation of life. But there are also some residual scars, even in the most resilient individuals.[7]

However, I believe that a larger sampling of the population of war children would show a deeper emotional and spiritual scarring than what is recorded currently, which constitutes a hidden core pain or soul sickness. With this generation of children aging into their '60s and '70s, it is imperative that large studies be conducted by national and international organizations to extract accurate information of the psychological, emotional, and spiritual consequences that resulted from the wars. In addition, studies need to determine how the future generations were influenced by these events.

Children became war orphans in several ways. First, their fathers were killed fighting the war. Also, there are the children in England that were sent into the countryside for their safety, only to discover later that their parents were killed in bomb attacks. There was the rescue of Jewish children, prior to the outbreak of World War II, in which they were placed onto kindertransport trains and sent to other countries. The United Kingdom took in nearly 10,000 predominantly Jewish children from Nazi Germany, Austria, Czechoslovakia, Poland and the free city of Danzig. These children were placed in British foster homes and hostels, and on farms. Lastly, there were the thousands of illegitimate children born to native mothers and occupying military soldiers. In some countries, the shame and embarrassment caused by fraternizing with the soldiers resulted in birth records being kept secret or suddenly become missing in the archives. Governments adopted postwar child welfare policies that emphasized the importance of purification of the future generations of the country by evacuating war children to other countries.

Separating children from their parents was not something new.

During the first part of the nineteenth century, hundreds of thousands of children were abandoned each year due to poverty and the harsh working conditions for women. About 1850, saving lives of these children became an urgent national issue because of fear of depopulation. Foundling hospitals were established and public agencies (often working with the church with the intent of preventing infanticide) became the supporting fathers. The prohibiting of paternity searches left the biological fathers free of responsibility for their out of wedlock children. The practice of separating children from mothers who were seen unfit long preceded World War II. In 1918, after the end of the country's civil war, 20,000 children of Finnish socialists and revolutionaries were taken from their mothers and brought into custody of child welfare organizations. Evacuation or exiling children in Britain by private charity organizations operated for some time before the outbreak of World War I. They made an industry of searching out foundlings and poor children and shipping them off to the colonies, "for a fresh start," as it was put. The child emigration from Britain also served a eugenic purpose. By sending off British children, the future white stock for the populations of the British Empire would be secured. By separating mother and child, state authorities were protecting both the children and the future of the nation.

By the end of World War I, moving German and Austrian children abroad started. About half a million children were moved to countries such as Switzerland, Denmark, Sweden, Holland, and Norway

Between 1939 and 1944 there were 70,000 Finish children sent off to Sweden. In Norway there was a national hate instilled into the morale of the country of native mothers with German fathers. They were treated as German sluts and beaten, not allowed to work, and looked down on by society. Their children were called German Bastards and not allowed citizenship. Norway sent thousands of them to Germany as a solution to the war child problem. In the Norwegian debate it was argued that the proposed exiling of the war children would not only "clean" the country of the offspring of the enemy, but would also save the children from the hate and persecution which would be their certain fate.

The Greek government told the world that children of communists were forced or kidnapped from their homes and transferred to neighboring communist countries to be brought up as future communist.[8]

By the end of the war, about 13 million children in Europe were facing destitution, poverty, and hunger. These were children whose parents had been killed or who had been abandoned, kidnapped, or deported. Each country established own policies on how to deal with the war child problem. When perceived as a national issue, with dire consequences for the future, governments took action to resolve the "war child problem."

When perceived as nothing but an ordinary social problem of poverty, illegitimacy, and related issues, governments took little interest in the welfare of these children. The children's immediate needs for food, love, and protection did not receive attention. Children of enemy or occupation soldiers were especially vulnerable to this lack of interest in the child as "being." When public interest lacked or vanished, silence, shame, and neglect fell upon the children.[9]

The war child welfare policies of each individual country are too extensive to present here, but they are well presented in "Children of World War II, the Hidden Enemy Legacy" by Kjersti Ericsson. The countries of Norway, Denmark, Germany, Spain, and France, and the occupied eastern territories and others all had their individual approach to solving the war child problem. Suffice it to say that there was a significant paradigm shift that occurred due to the welfare of these children. The emotional and spiritual makeup of generations of children from these war orphans was significantly impacted by these events. Many may have developed into orphan hearts. Many are still looking for their fathers or records of them to regain their true identity and family name.

The Forgotten Fatherless

These are stories of orphans from World War II. They became the next generation of teenagers and parents that would change the culture of the world. They were the casualties of emotional depravation that many experienced during their childhood development, including lack of affirmation, lack of being loved, and lack of being told that they were lovable; lack of a safe haven, fear, abandonment, belonging to no one and no country.

Memories of a German War Orphan

My Story—Karin Janin

I was born in Ansbach, Germany, during a time when the Germans were trying to rebuild their country after World War II. Immediately after birth, I was placed in an orphanage, never to know that first loving embrace of a caring mother or a proud father's smile.

My first four years were spent in an unloving environment, an environment torn by the war. By the time I reached the age of four, I was still unable to chew food because I had only been given pabulum.

I was introduced to my new family on Christmas Eve 1950... no longer lived in confinement, wondering where the next meal would come from, looking out a window and wishing for a better life. The Russell family had money, lots of money, lots of food, and most of all, lots of love.... Fear of abandonment was never far away, but it seemed to subside with this family. My adopted father was my hero and would call me his "Little Princess." I felt so special.

Dad (a title I gladly learned to use) taught me my most valuable lesson in life: that lesson was UNCONDITIONAL LOVE. He showed me how to treat others with respect and how to make everyone feel special. I was happy for the first time in my life, for I belonged to a family unit. It didn't matter where they were from, it only mattered that they wanted me. I thought my life was perfect and that it would go on forever. I had everything a child could ever want including love, so much love, something an orphan can never get enough of. After living this Cinderella life for a few years, my beloved father had a heart attack and died suddenly. My knight in shining armor was gone and life was forever changed...

For awhile my brother and I lived in Kirbyville, Texas, with my grandmother, Mama's Mama. Mama's Mama was a tough disciplinarian. She believed in the use of small, thin tree branches if you did something that she disapproved of. Ruth Russell eventually remarried. This was NOT a match made in Heaven. During the first few years of their marriage, we lived in Houston, Texas. Ruth had lived a glamorous life while her husband, on the other hand, came from a lower middle class, cold, and strict English background. Ruth's second husband was verbally abusive to her. I would sometimes go outside at night and sing my heart out. Or gaze at the stars for answers. Sometimes I would pretend that a UFO would whisk me away from all the sadness and tension. My high school years should have been my happiest, but they were not. The tension kept getting worse and worse with the years.

The Forgotten Fatherless

After graduating from high school, I attended Lamar University in Beaumont, Texas. I was not particularly interested in studying just in boys, boys, boys. I attended several colleges within a span of 1 ½ years and finally gave up. I quit college and became a stewardess...for Delta Airlines.... What a blast! I burned the candle at both ends. Men, men, men. Dates, dates, dates, dates. I was totally clueless about the world at large, but I was having fun! I fell hopelessly in love with Paul. He will always be someone very special in my heart for we shared a special love. He was raised in an interfaith environment. His mother was Methodist and his father was Jewish. It made no difference to me; he was the love of my life.

My parents, on the other hand, could not accept his religious background, for they were staunch Southern Baptist. I began to show signs of an emotional breakdown. I was emotionally torn apart. I wanted to please everyone and at the same time, I wanted to love Paul, and that our love be accepted! Paul ended the relationship because he could see what it was doing to me emotionally. Shortly after that I was placed in a hospital for I almost died of an internal bleeding ulcer. I wanted to die, my true love was gone, he wouldn't even visit me in the hospital. I felt betrayed by my parents, my religious leader, my church, and mostly abandoned by Paul.

Life was depressing. I moved to Houston, Texas, caring very little about my life. Worked as a receptionist and met my future husband. He proposed marriage to me, we sealed the proposal one night, and I became pregnant–classic story. We went to a border town in Mexico and I had an abortion. It was a horrible experience, one that I will never forget. My self esteem was at an all time low and I cared very little about my future. I was ashamed and embarrassed, and at the same time, I was impressed that the man who paid for my abortion, the father of his unborn child, still wanted to marry me. I thought this was what love was all about; it didn't matter that I didn't love him, but that he loved me. Seven years later,

13

this very man threw the abortion in my face. He conveniently forgot that the abortion was a joint decision.

I married a cold man. Somehow, we managed to have three beautiful children. Ten years later, we divorced because he was verbally abusive. The verbal abuse went on daily, sometimes all day long. The better I felt about myself, the more he felt threatened. He never ran around on me, he was always home, but we never communicated. His only form of communication was criticism. According to him, I was too stupid to do anything. After ten years of putting up with his verbal abuse, I felt it was time to move on. I knew that I could not change him, but I could change myself.

I continued to enter relationships that were emotionally abusive. It seemed I was quite comfortable with that type of relationship. It took a while to realize the pattern I had developed.

When I was adopted, my name was changed from Karin Janin to Karen Ruth. Years later, I decided to formally go back to the original spelling of my first and middle name. I had no idea why I felt it necessary to do this, but that night I had a painfully revealing dream explaining what had happened to me while I was in the orphanage. The dream narrator showed me a picture of myself during those early years. It was a distorted picture of a child who had been physically abused and was very, very frightened. Then the dream narrator said, "This was what happened to you; this was you."

I woke up feeling a great relief that some of my past had been revealed, for I had always wondered what those first four years of my life were like. I spent the day crying, releasing, and crying more. I couldn't stop crying. I believe that was the most significant dream I've ever had. That day, I was able to let go of the past forever. I was no longer angry I understood the significance of the dream. The past is over all we have is the present and future.

No matter how rough my journey has been, I always kept that inner light burning. I knew that I was not taken out of the orphanage to be forgotten by the Universe, that there was purpose in my living. I realize that problems are simply opportunities for growth![10]

Reflections of American World War II Orphans

Bill

What happened is our family had no males. All of that generation and the previous generation had been killed off, except for one uncle. So there were no males around, and I think it had a pretty strong effect on us.... We gathered views that were all female views. We didn't gather views that were male. Then, in addition to that, I was very used to having women tell me what to do. It was a matriarchal society. I had real difficulties in getting along with a male. I had difficulty making eye contact with them. I even look at my son, and I think, "Jesus, the effect is reaching to him." Because of my role as a father and that extends to the relationship I had with his mother, he's had a troubled youth.[11]

Eric

My mother and I had our problems, just whatever, a mother-son relationship compounded by a very strong, very domineering woman. The other side is I have difficulties in relationships with men. I had no brothers to relate to, and even though I had my uncle and my stepfather, I would never let myself get completely close to men out of loyalty to my father. Even though my father was dead, and they were father figures, I would never completely open up to, or would treat, another man like a father.[12]

Clint

I always felt that I was a loner. When it came to getting into fights, which kids will do, I would avoid them. I should have just gone ahead and fought and been a boy, but I wasn't. I felt as a result of avoiding fights I was somewhat picked on. They said things like, "Yeah, your father was a big war hero, but you're sure not!"

My mother, she always had these very high standards. I always felt like I had to live up to the image of my father. This was an impossible task because of her feelings about him, that he could do no wrong. I think I could have been a lot better father. I devoted too much of my time to work and my career. I thought number one was my job. I should have spent a lot more time being more family oriented. I was raised without a father image or a figure as to what a father should be.

I live on the edge. If I have a dime I'll spend it. I have never been able to save money. I am a risk taker, a gambler in many ways, risky stocks and lottery tickets. I smoked and drank to the point where I can't do that anymore.... I always drive very fast.[13]

Jim

I became, at a very young age, the man of the house. That was the beginning of the end for me and created problems for the rest of my life. My grandmother was basically right about my mother's weaknesses as a parent. Actually, the war was the basic problem. If my father hadn't been killed in the war, I probably wouldn't have been trashed. But we don't know for sure what that would have been like. But I have no doubt I had something taken away from me. I didn't get to grow up like everyone else. Not only did I not have my father, I had to take care of my mother. I learned how to take care of me, too. So I became close to myself and I projected this strength to everybody.[14]

A Fatherless World War II Child from Britain

Thinking back to my childhood in bombed out London, being shunted from one homeless centre to another. Mum not knowing where the next meal was coming from, no family to turn to for help, and eventually marrying someone who was not a bad man, but was unable to show me any sort of affection whatsoever. We were eventually given a council flat in South London. I remember sharing a bedroom with my half brother, and my step father would creep in after finishing work and take my brother out of the bedroom to play with whatever new toy he had bought for him. I would just lay there thinking, "Why does he never buy anything for me?" Not knowing then that he wasn't my dad. Then one particular night he said, "Angela are you awake, I've got something for you." I was just so excited when he handed me a little man made of beads with bendy arms and legs. The excitement was so much that as I was bending the arms and legs in all directions, the whole thing just fell to bits. I was devastated and I heard him saying to Mum, "See, that's why I never give her anything."

I eventually started to think that maybe I was bad and undeserving, and then, as I got a bit older, this changed to a complete dislike of my step father, so when Mum eventually told me at the age of twelve that he wasn't my real dad, I was overjoyed! This euphoria was short lived; I became a victim of sorrow. Why did I not have a real dad to love me, to kiss me goodnight, to give me encouragement and tell me how precious I was. How I yearned for all those things, the hurt was indescribable.

When I reached my teens, all I wanted was to get away and find someone who would really love me, so at the tender age of sixteen I became pregnant, quit college to get married; and for me that was it. I'm just an ordinary Mum who has brought up four children, had no career, and only now at this late stage in my life am I starting to find my feet and gain a bit of confidence.[15]

More Recent Examples

Even to this day the spiritual warfare continues. As long as there are orphan hearts created in this world, God's children will be kept from truly knowing and experiencing the love of the Father's heart.

Wednesday, 18 June, 2003. In northern Uganda, well armed rebels of the Lord's Resistance Army attacked an orphanage at around 24:00 local time, from where they abducted Sudanese and Ugandan children. The United Nations Children's Fund estimates that during the past year, over 5,000 civilians have been abducted by the LRA. According to Sacred Heart sisters who run the orphanage in the northern Ugandan town of Adjumani, less than 40 kilometers from the Sudanese border, the rebels abducted 16 Sudanese and Ugandan orphans between the ages of seven and 15. After taking them from their dormitories, the children were beaten, tied together with ropes, and then marched off into the bush. While the boys are turned into ruthless killers, the girls are often given out to senior rebel officers and forced to become their wives.[16]

"No Happy End in Sight for Russia's Many Orphans"
The Russia Journal

The country's various orphanages, shelters, and boarding schools are home to over half a million children. Of these, few are even orphans in the literal sense of the word (that is, children who have lost both parents). Most fall into the category of "social orphans," children who have been abandoned by their parents or whose parents have lost their parental rights. But regardless of how they came to be in state care, the majority of orphaned children meet a similarly bleak fate. Most children's homes are overcrowded and underfunded; up to 300 children of various ages may be living under the same roof. The result of such circumstances can be horrific: at least 5,000 children end up in court each year, another 3,000 become street children, and 1,500 commit suicide.[17]

Nordic Journal of African Studies
Sixteen million children were newly orphaned in 2003. Wars orphaned or separated 1 million children from their families in the 1990s.[18]

Chosen by Grace Orphan & Adoption Ministry
Two to five percent of refuges worldwide are kids living without parents. 17.5 million are 0- 5 years old, 47 million are 6-11 years old, and 79 million are 12-17 years old. 87.6 million are in Asia, 43.4 million are in Sub-Saharan Africa, 12.4 million are in Latin America and the Caribbean, 1.5 million are in Central and Eastern Europe. 800,000 pass through America's foster care system each year.[19]

UNICEF estimates the number of orphans at approximately 210 million.

Nordic Journal of African Studies
One of the major effects of the HIV/AIDS pandemic in Malawi, as in Sub-Sahara Africa in general, is the rising number of orphans. In 1999, UNAIDS estimated that some 390,000 children in Malawi had been orphaned due to deaths caused by HIV/AIDS1. Family relations are becoming more elastic and are sometimes overstretched to accommodate the vulnerable members. The degree of success depends on multiple factors that include: the material conditions of the respective families, the level of integration of the orphans in the new social relationships, the ages and gender of the orphans, the size of the family

in which they are found, the willingness of the family members to accommodate more people – as well as the intentions of doing so – and the degree of vulnerability of the orphans themselves. The last includes multiple loss of family members, especially over a short period, the type of loss (status, property, etc.), being physically alienated from one's original home through relocation, disability, and lack of trust in the guardian(s).[20]

Statistics from the Centers of Disease Control and Prevention (CDC), Interagency Forum of Child and Family Statistics, Criminal Justice and Behavior:

✓ 63% of all youth suicides come from fatherless homes.
✓ 90% of homeless and runaway children are from fatherless homes.
✓ 80% of rapists are motivated by displaced anger and come from fatherless homes.
✓ 71% of all high school dropouts come from fatherless homes.
✓ 70% of juveniles come from fatherless homes.
✓ 85% of youths sitting in prison grew up in fatherless homes.
✓ 2 out of 5 children in the United States do not live with a father.
    If you come from a fatherless home, you are 4.6 times more likely to commit suicide, 6.6 times more likely to become a teenage mother, 24 times more likely to run away, 15 times more likely to have behavior disorders, 6.3 times more likely to end up in a state operated institution, and 10.8 times more likely to commit rape.[21]

This epidemic festers into the very core of society unfettered and rampant. Without an antidote, it will continue to spread increasing in degrees of severity.

Chapter One
Where the Orphan Heart Disposition Began

Many examples of the orphan heart's beginnings are described in the Old Testament. This chapter, are compiles relevant passages that expound on the history of orphan heart disposition and provide explications of each example.

LUCIFER

Some scholars contend that Lucifer was the first to experience an orphan heart. He had a special relationship with God. God created Satan and other angelic beings with free will to be his heavenly children.

> How are you fallen from heaven, O Lucifer, son of the morning! How are you cut down to the ground, which did weaken the nations! For you have said in your heart, I will ascend into heaven, I will exalt my throne above the stars of God: I will sit also on the mount of the congregation, in the sides of the north: I will ascend above the heights of the clouds; I will make myself like the Most High. If we accept that the anointed cherub, son of the morning, and morning

star all refer to Satan than we can conclude that Satan had a special place of honor guarding the throne of God. However, because of his pride, he rebelled against authority. He rejected parental authority, he separated himself from the Father by wanting to take over control and do things his way *(Isaiah 14:14)*.

He replied, "I saw Satan fall like lightning from heaven." *(Luke 10:18 NIV)*.

In his book, *Spiritual Slavery to Spiritual Sonship*, Jack Frost contends:

> Lucifer became the ultimate spiritual orphan. Separated from his original home, he became resentful toward anyone who enjoyed intimacy with Father God, particularly those human beings God created in His own image. Because he no longer walked in Father's mission of love, Lucifer began to compete for a place of recognition, position, and power.
>
> Jealousy drove Lucifer to deceive Adam and Eve. The tool to cripple mankind and weaken the nations was orphan thinking. His strategy was to convince man to think the way he did, homeless and cut off from God's love, and thereby weaken man to the point where he would give in to temptation and allow shame and fear to replace intimacy.
>
> Satan's thoughts were, "I will do it my way. I will pursue the things that make me feel good and give me a sense of value and significance!" And because Adam and Eve bought into his orphan thinking, they, as well as we, have received his orphan heart as part of the "package deal."[22]
>
> The quickest way to shut down intimacy and trust is by sowing seeds of doubt into the relationship. Appearing in the form of a serpent, Lucifer approached Eve and led her to question God's character and integrity.[23]

However, this may not be the first instance of an orphan heart. There is a view that Satan was cast out of Heaven after Adam and Eve were created, because God said the Creation was still "very good" on the 6th day after he had created man. Satan had not fallen yet. One opinion from the blog http://jesus-loves-u.blogspot.com/2007/08/when-did-satan-fall-from-heaven.html, posted on Wednesday, August 29, 2007, states:

> Satan did not fall until after the creation, maybe even one hundred or so years later. All that we know is Adam was one hundred thirty when Seth was born. That is the first date given in Scripture. Before Seth, they had Cain and Abel, but dates are not given. Before he had Cain and Abel, they were removed from the garden. Therefore, it would have been somewhere around a hundred years during which time Satan may have become jealous of the fellowship that Adam and Eve enjoyed with God. Satan may have observed their relationship for one hundred years, and said, "Hey, I want them to worship me! I want to rule humanity. I want to walk with them in the garden. I will ascend unto the high heavens. I will take over the seat of the Most High. I will, I will, I will."

ADAM AND EVE
The Creation of Man and Woman

Then God said, "Let Us make man in Our image, according to Our likeness; and let them rule over the fish of the sea and over the birds of the sky and over the cattle and over all the earth, and over every creeping thing that creeps on the earth." God created man in His own image, in the image of God He created him; male and female He created them *(Genesis 1:26-27)*.

Then the LORD God formed man of dust from the ground, and breathed into his nostrils the breath of life (could this be actually a kiss from the Father?); and man became a living being. (Adam is being loved by the love of the Father pouring into his soul) The LORD God planted a garden toward the east, in Eden; and there He placed the man whom He had formed out of the ground. The LORD God caused to grow every tree that is pleasing to the sight and good for food; the tree of life also in the midst of the garden, and the tree of the knowledge of good and evil *(Genesis 2:7-9)*.

Then the LORD God took the man and put him into the Garden of Eden to cultivate it and keep it. And the LORD God commanded the man, "You are free to eat from any tree in the garden; but you must not eat from the tree of the knowledge of good and evil, for when you eat of it you will surely die." *(Genesis 2:15-17)*.

So the LORD God caused a deep sleep to fall upon the man, and he slept; then He took one of his ribs and closed up the flesh at that place. The LORD God fashioned into a woman the rib which He had taken from the man, and brought her to the man. The man said, "This is now bone of my bones, and flesh of my flesh; she shall be called Woman, because she was taken out of Man *(Genesis 2:21-23)*.

Separation from God

God put the tree of knowledge of good and evil in the Garden of Eden to give Adam and Eve a choice—to obey Him or disobey Him. Adam and Eve were free to do anything they wanted, except eat from the tree of knowledge of good and evil. If God had not given Adam and Eve the choice, they would have essentially been robots, simply doing what they were programmed to do. God created Adam and Eve to be "free" beings, able to make decisions, able to choose between good and evil. In order for Adam and Eve to truly be "free"—they had to have a choice.[24]

There was nothing essentially evil about the tree or the fruit of the tree. It is unlikely that eating the fruit truly gave Adam and Eve any further knowledge. It was the act of disobedience that opened Adam and Eve's eyes to evil. Their sin of disobeying God brought sin and evil into the world and into their lives. Eating the fruit, as an act of disobedience against God, was what gave Adam and Eve knowledge of evil.

When the woman saw that the fruit of the tree was good for food and pleasing to the eye, and also desirable for gaining wisdom, she took some and ate it *(Genesis 3:6)*.

Notice that when she ate nothing happened.

She also gave some to her husband, who was with her, and he ate it. Then the eyes of both of them were opened, and they realized they were naked; so they sewed fig leaves together and made coverings for themselves *(Genesis 3:6-7)*.

Until he ate, their eyes were not opened to evil. This was because they were one.

God did not want Adam and Eve to sin. God knew ahead of time what the results of sin would be. God knew that Adam and Eve would sin, and would thereby bring evil, suffering, and death into the world. Why, then, did God put the tree in the Garden of Eden and allow Satan to tempt Adam and Eve? God put the tree of knowledge of good and evil in the Garden of Eden to give Adam and Eve a choice. God allowed Satan to tempt Adam and Eve to force them to make the choice. Adam and Eve chose, of their own free wills, to disobey God and eat the forbidden fruit. The result—evil, sin, suffering, sickness, and death have plagued the world ever since. Adam and Eve's decision results in each and every person being born with a sin nature, a tendency to sin. Adam and Eve's decision is what ultimately required Jesus Christ to die on the cross and shed His blood on our behalf. Through faith in Christ, we can be free from sin's consequences, and ultimately free from sin itself.[25]

God created his son Adam to be with him in perfect love, to feel secure, to provide Adams every need, to have a perfect intimate relationship with him as Father and son. When He created Eve as his daughter, she too had the same loving relationship with the Father. However, Satan was now in rebellion with God the Father, and when he came to Eve in the Garden of Eden, it was familiar territory to him.

You have been in Eden the garden of God; every precious stone was your covering, the sardius, topaz, and the diamond, the beryl, the onyx, and the jasper, the sapphire, the emerald, and the carbuncle, and gold: the workmanship of your tabrets and of your pipes was prepared in you in the day that you were created *(Ezekiel 28:13)*.

(According to *The Complete Word Study Old Testament*, the word "covering" is from the Hebrew word *cakak*, and means "to cover over, protect, defend.")

From the time of Satan's fall, his major goal has been to destroy the family unit especially the family relationship of humans with God. He does this through the establishment of an orphan heart within us. He will do whatever possible to destroy the father's influence in a family, thereby altering the children's image of God. World wars have been part of his means to accomplish this goal. In the history of mankind, spiritual cultures have been altered because of these wars. Altering our image of God fractures the possibility of intimacy that Father God wants to have with us as His sons and daughters.

In addition, Satan has some unholy scheme to destroy femininity because of his contempt and absolute hatred of woman. He will do anything to degrade and deface her femininity because this represents the nurturing nature of God. Many religions place their women under heavy veils of oppression and even perpetuate acts of violence against them. Female circumcision occurs in some African cultures. Young girls are mutilated to keep them from being consumed by sexual passions later in life. In some Middle Eastern countries, women are often blamed and punished when their husbands commit acts of adultery. For centuries, Satan has had this special hatred for women. He has sought to destroy and devalue femininity in the hearts of humankind since the day in the Garden of Eden when the Lord God gave the women the power to defeat him.

> And the LORD God said to the serpent, Because you have done this, you are cursed above all cattle, and above every beast of the field; on your belly shall you go, and dust shall you eat all the days of your life. And I will put enmity between you and the woman, and between your seed and her seed; he shall bruise you on the head, and you shall bruise him on the heel *(Genesis 3:14-15)*.

What was it like to be in the Garden with God? There was an incredible agape love of the Father for His children and an incredible love of the children for the Father. There was no fear, shame, rejection, feelings of abandonment, feelings of being unloved, unwanted, sadness, loneliness, etc. There was unconditional love, total peace, absolute security, absolute safety, absolute confidence, absolute joy, and perfection beyond belief.

As James Jordan states on his FatherHeart Ministries DVD, "The Orphan Spirit":

> Because of God's love for them, He could not allow them to eat from the tree of life forever and He banished them. God could see sin was going to make man depraved, depressed, hopeless, despaired, and sorrowful. They would never know God's love again as they had known. Separated from God's agape love must have been incredible sorrow and pain. He physically drove them out. This was the first major paradigm shift from sonship to orphan. They now experienced the emotion of a broken heart more painful than any human being has ever known. To have to be separated from an incredible love. Walking out of the Garden and out of the Father's agape love. Eros love now entered into the world. What came into their hearts was that they became fatherless. They became more like the one who was cast out of heaven. There was now more of a union, similarity, and oneness with Satan. There became an unholy alliance between two orphan spirits. The orphan spirit of Satan and the orphan spirit that came down upon the human race. As Adam and Eve walked out of the garden, everyone of us was in them.[26]

We are the fruit of their seed. Now the man called his wife's name Eve, because she was the mother of all the living *(Genesis 3:20).*

Paradise was now lost and the perfect love broken. Shame came into the world.

When the woman saw that the tree was good for food, and that it was a delight to the eyes, and that the tree was desirable to make one wise, she took from its fruit and ate; and she gave also to her husband with her, and he ate. Then the eyes of both of them were opened, and they knew that they were naked; and they sewed fig leaves together and made themselves loin coverings. The love, protection, and the Father providing for their every need was gone *(Genesis 3:6-7)*.

For God knows that in the day you eat from it your eyes will be opened, and you will be like God, knowing good and evil *(Genesis 3:5)*.

Then the LORD God said to the woman, "What is this you have done?" And the woman said, "The serpent deceived me, and I ate." *(Genesis 3:13)*.

Then the LORD God said, "Behold, the man has become like one of Us, knowing good and evil; and now, he might stretch out his hand, and take also from the tree of life, and eat, and live forever." Therefore the LORD God sent him out from the Garden of Eden, to cultivate the ground from which he was taken *(Genesis 3:22-23)*.

Cursed is the ground because of you; in toil you will eat of it All the days of your life. Both thorns and thistles it shall grow for you; And you will eat the plants of the field; By the sweat of your face You will eat bread, Till you return to the ground, Because from it you were taken; For you are dust, And to dust you shall return *(Genesis 3:17-19)*.

Abandonment and rejection entered into the world. So also, loneliness, sorrow, outcast, mistrust, and all other emotions of being an orphan and fatherless. The orphan heart was established.[27]

This may have caused a great pain in the heart of God for the human race. He sent prophets and poets to convey his heart to the people. But no one could do it until he sent his Son, who would reveal the heart of the Father exactly as the Father wanted it revealed to a lost world, an orphan world.[28]

He who has seen Me has seen the Father; how can you say, "Show us the Father"? Do you not believe that I am in the Father, and the Father is in Me? The words that I say to you I do not speak on My own initiative, but the Father abiding in Me does His works *(John 14:9-10)*.

The Father is expressing his heart: I will not leave you as orphans; I will come to you. *(John 14:18)*.

Christianity—most consider it about getting saved, getting full of the Holy Spirit, and going out and doing miracles, preaching the gospel. However, Christianity is about a Father who lost his children and it broke his heart and he simply wants them back. So God so loved the world he sent his only begotten son. Jesus died on the cross because his Father loves us and because he loved his Father. It is about a Father whose heart is broken to an orphan world and all he wants to do is come to you and me in Jesus' name and open our eyes to see his Father's love for us.[29]

ISHMAEL AND ISAAC
The Circumstances of Ishmael's Birth
(Genesis 16:1-16)

Abram marries Agar
Now Sarai, Abram's wife had borne him no children, and she had an Egyptian maid whose name was Hagar. So Sarai said to Abram, "Now behold, the LORD has prevented me from bearing children. Please go in to my maid; perhaps I will obtain children through her." And Abram listened to the voice of Sarai. After Abram had lived ten years in the land of Canaan, Abram's wife Sarai took Hagar the Egyptian, her maid, and gave her to her husband Abram as his wife. He went in to Hagar, and she conceived; and when she saw that she had conceived, her mistress was despised in her sight.

Hagar flees from Sarai

And Sarai said to Abram, "May the wrong done me be upon you. I gave my maid into your arms, but when she saw that she had conceived, I was despised in her sight. May the LORD judge between you and me." But Abram said to Sarai, "Behold, your maid is in your power; do to her what is good in your sight." So Sarai treated her harshly, and she fled from her presence.

An angel tells Hagar to return to Sarai

Now the angel of the LORD found her by a spring of water in the wilderness, by the spring on the way to Shur. He said, "Hagar, Sarai's maid, where have you come from and where are you going?" And she said, "I am fleeing from the presence of my mistress Sarai." Then the angel of the LORD said to her, "Return to your mistress, and submit yourself to her authority." Moreover, the angel of the LORD said to her, "I will greatly multiply your descendants so that they will be too many to count." The angel of the LORD said to her further, "Behold, you are with child, And you will bear a son; And you shall call his name Ishmael, Because the LORD has given heed to your affliction. He will be a wild donkey of a man, His hand will be against everyone, And everyone's hand will be against him; And he will live to the east of all his brothers." Then she called the name of the LORD who spoke to her, "You are a God who sees," for she said, "Have I even remained alive here after seeing Him?" Therefore the well was called Beer lahai roi; behold, it is between Kadesh and Bered.

Birth of Ismael

So Hagar bore Abram a son; and Abram called the name of his son, whom Hagar bore, Ishmael. 16 Abram was eighty-six years old when Hagar bore Ishmael to him

Abraham and the Covenant of Circumcision
(Genesis 17:1-21)

Abram becomes Abraham

Now when Abram was ninety-nine years old, the LORD appeared to Abram and said to him, "I am God Almighty; Walk before Me, and be blameless. I will establish My covenant between Me and you, And I will multiply you exceedingly." Abram fell on his face, and God talked with him, saying, "As for Me, behold, My covenant is with you, And you will be the father of a multitude of nations. No longer shall your name be called Abram, But your name shall be Abraham; For I have made you the father of a multitude of nations. I will make you exceedingly fruitful, and I will make nations of you, and kings will come forth from you. I will establish My covenant between Me and you and your descendants after you throughout their generations for an everlasting covenant, to be God to you and to your descendants after you. I will give to you and to your descendants after you, the land of your sojournings, all the land of Canaan, for an everlasting possession; and I will be their God."

Sarai becomes Sara

Then God said to Abraham, "As for Sarai your wife, you shall not call her name Sarai, but Sarah shall be her name. I will bless her, and indeed I will give you a son by her. Then I will bless her, and she shall be a mother of nations; kings of peoples will come from her."

Isaac is promised by God

Then Abraham fell on his face and laughed, and said in his heart, "Will a child be born to a man one hundred years old? And will Sarah, who is ninety years old, bear a child?" And Abraham said to God, "Oh that Ishmael might live before You!" But God said, "No, but Sarah your wife will bear you a son, and you shall call his name Isaac; and I will establish My covenant with him for an everlasting covenant for his descendants after him. "As for Ishmael, I have heard you; behold, I will bless him, and will make him fruitful and will multiply him exceedingly. He shall become the father of twelve princes, and I will make him a great nation. But My covenant I will establish with Isaac, whom Sarah will bear to you at this season next year."

Birth of Isaac Promised
(Genesis 18:1-14)

Three strangers visit Abraham
Now the LORD appeared to him by the oaks of Mamre, while he was sitting at the tent door in the heat of the day. When he lifted up his eyes and looked, behold, three men were standing opposite him; and when he saw them, he ran from the tent door to meet them and bowed himself to the earth, and said, "My Lord, if now I have found favor in Your sight, please do not pass Your servant by. Please let a little water be brought and wash your feet, and rest yourselves under the tree; and I will bring a piece of bread, that you may refresh yourselves; after that you may go on, since you have visited your servant." And they said, "So do, as you have said." So Abraham hurried into the tent to Sarah, and said, "Quickly, prepare three measures of fine flour, knead it and make bread cakes." Abraham also ran to the herd, and took a tender and choice calf and gave it to the servant, and he hurried to prepare it. He took curds and milk and the calf which he had prepared, and placed it before them; and he was standing by them under the tree as they ate.

A son is promised to Sara
Then they said to him, "Where is Sarah your wife?" And he said, "There, in the tent." He said, "I will surely return to you at this time next year; and behold, Sarah your wife will have a son." And Sarah was listening at the tent door, which was behind him. Now Abraham and Sarah were old, advanced in age; Sarah was past childbearing. Sarah laughed to herself, saying, "After I have become old, shall I have pleasure, my lord being old also?" And the LORD said to Abraham, "Why did Sarah laugh, saying, 'Shall I indeed bear a child, when I am so old?' Is anything too difficult for the LORD? At the appointed time I will return to you, at this time next year, and Sarah will have a son."

Isaac Is Born
(Genesis 21:1-14)

The birth of Isaac
Then the LORD took note of Sarah as He had said, and the LORD did for Sarah as He had promised. So Sarah conceived and bore a son to Abraham in his old age, at the appointed time of which God had spoken to him. Abraham called the name of his son who was born to him, whom Sarah bore to him, Isaac. Then Abraham circumcised his son Isaac when he was eight days old, as God had commanded him. Now Abraham was one hundred years old when his son Isaac was born to him. Sarah said, "God has made laughter for me; everyone who hears will laugh with me." And she said, "Who would have said to Abraham that Sarah would nurse children? Yet I have borne him a son in his old age." The child grew and was weaned, and Abraham made a great feast on the day that Isaac was weaned.

Hagar and Ishmael driven out
Now Sarah saw the son of Hagar the Egyptian, whom she had borne to Abraham, mocking. Therefore she said to Abraham, "Drive out this maid and her son, for the son of this maid shall not be an heir with my son Isaac." The matter distressed Abraham greatly because of his son. But God said to Abraham, "Do not be distressed because of the lad and your maid; whatever Sarah tells you, listen to her, for through Isaac your descendants shall be named. And of the son of the maid I will make a nation also, because he is your descendant." So Abraham rose early in the morning and took bread and a skin of water and gave them to Hagar, putting them on her shoulder, and gave her the boy, and sent her away. And she departed and wandered about in the wilderness of Beersheba

Notice the similarity here to Adam and Eve. The father physically removes the son and throws him out, thereby making the son fatherless, an orphan. No longer was he safe in the father's love, secure in his home, affirmed by his father's love. The son was now abandoned, rejected, ashamed, feeling sadness, sorrow, etc.—all the feelings that an orphan heart will go through.

The Story of Hagar and Ishmael
(Genesis 21:15-21)

When the water in the skin was used up, she left the boy under one of the bushes. Then she went and sat down opposite him, about a bowshot away, for she said, "Do not let me see the boy die." And she sat opposite him, and lifted up her voice and wept.

God protects Hagar and Ishmael
God heard the lad crying; and the angel of God called to Hagar from heaven and said to her, "What is the matter with you, Hagar? Do not fear, for God has heard the voice of the lad where he is. Arise, lift up the lad, and hold him by the hand, for I will make a great nation of him." Then God opened her eyes and she saw a well of water; and she went and filled the skin with water and gave the lad a drink. God was with the lad, and he grew; and he lived in the wilderness and became an archer. He lived in the wilderness of Paran, and his mother took a wife for him from the land of Egypt.

In one of her sermons, Reverend Judy Landt, Vernon Presbyterian Church, elucidates the story further.

God had promised Abraham and Sarah that they would produce a great nation of many descendants, but the birth of their son Isaac turned out to be twenty-five years in the future. As is often the way with people, Sarah was tired of waiting and decided to take control of the situation herself. The ancient world offered an alternative for women unable to conceive. Sarah suggests to Abraham that he spend the night with Hagar, her Egyptian servant girl. If Hagar produces a child, it will be considered Sarah's child. Problem solved, or so Sarah thought. Of course, things were not so simple. As soon as Hagar's pregnancy becomes apparent, Sarah's jealousy begins to arise. Conveniently forgetting that she herself encouraged the event that led to Hagar's pregnancy, she blames Abraham for taking her up on the offer.

"You should have known I didn't really mean it," I imagine her telling Abraham. "She's been insulting me since the minute you got her pregnant, and you've done absolutely nothing to stop it."

Abraham, I'm sure, was perplexed at what the big deal was. "Sarah, this was all your idea to begin with. I'm sick and tired of all the whining and complaining around here. I need some peace and quiet. She's your servant girl, you deal with it," he tells Sarah, "and please, don't tell me what you did." Well, that's all Sarah needed to hear—she becomes intolerable. "Hagar, get up and do your chores. Don't tell me you don't feel well, you're just being lazy. Get the laundry finished or you'll be sorry." "Feeling a little fat and unattractive today, Hagar? Get busy; it'll take your mind off your looks." Finally, Sarah's abuse takes its toll. Hagar runs away, into the desert. There God visits her, tells her to return to Sarah, and makes her a promise. Hagar will give birth to Ishmael. God will make her the mother of multitudes.[30]

In due course, Sarah gives birth to Abraham's child, Isaac. But the birth of their son Isaac turned out to be twenty-five years later. However, God's gift of a long awaited son did nothing to calm Sarah's jealousy and dislike of Hagar. If anything, the bad blood between the two of them increased. Every time Sarah set eyes on little Ishmael, she could feel the sour seeds of rage beginning to burn in the pit of her stomach. Now a mother herself, she has a new reason to be jealous. She wants her Isaac to rule the roost. He is, after all, the special child of God's covenant. God's chosen one should not suffer the indignity of having to compete with a slave girl's child for his father's inheritance, for his father's affection. Eventually Sarah's feelings bubble over like a giant volcano eruption, spewing burning lava everywhere. "Abraham," she announces, "get that woman and her son out of here. I mean it. I've had it with both of them, they need to go."

In what is certainly not his finest moment, Abraham agrees. Therefore, Hagar and Ishmael are sent off into the desert, with only a small quantity of bread and water to sustain them. It amounts to a death sentence. When their meager supplies run out, they face agonizing death by dehydration in the relentless desert heat. Hagar sits down a distance from her child, not wanting to watch him die.

This could easily be the sad the end of the story, but it is not. God intervenes on behalf of Hagar and Ishmael. Hagar hears the voice of God, saying, "Fear not, Hagar, God will take care of you and your son." Echoing the covenant with Abraham, God says, "God will make a great nation of Ishmael, too." Hagar's eyes are opened, she sees a well of water. The two drink from it, their lives are spared. And Hagar and Ishmael go on to live rich lives, blessed and cared for by God.

The good news: none of this stops God's work. No matter how badly we mess up, God seems to find a way. The covenants are fulfilled. Of course, how God goes about it can seem a little peculiar. Why, for example, does God convince Abraham to go along with Sarah's dreadful plan to send Hagar and Ishmael off to the desert, only to intervene later to prevent their deaths? The truth is, there is always more to God than we can understand. Sometimes we need to live with the ambiguity of God, and stop trying to make God simple. It's enough to know that God doesn't give up on us, and that the accomplishment of

God's purposes does not depend on our ability to be nice all the time. That's very good news we can gladly hear.

You know that both Jews and Christians claim Abraham, Sarah and Isaac as our ancestors in faith. Both Jews and Christians believe we have inherited God's promises to Abraham. These promises are central to both faith traditions.

We learn there is another side of God's family tree, the Abraham-Hagar-Ishmael side. And over a billion Muslims worldwide also trace their ancestry back to Abraham via Ishmael. Muslims claim God's promises to Hagar and Ishmael, promises almost identical to those claimed by Christians and Jews. I will make you a great nation. I will be your God. Muslims regard Abraham, who turned away from the idol worship of his ancestors to worship one God, as the first Muslim. He is also considered one of God's great prophets, perhaps not quite on a par with Mohammed, but close. The Koran, Islam's holy book, includes many references to Abraham's life that are also recorded in the Hebrew Bible, and many religious rituals practiced by Muslims are linked to Abraham.

All of which leads us to conclude that Christians, Jews, and Muslims worship the same God. The God known as Yahweh in the Hebrew Bible, the God of the New Testament whom we know in Jesus Christ, the God whom Muslims call Allah are one and the same. And God has promised to bless and protect both sides of the family tree.

Of course, it is human nature to want to claim God's blessings and promises for ourselves and others like us. It is human nature to create insiders and outsiders, and to treat the outsiders as though they were excluded from the circle of God's love. We saw it happen with Sarah. She wants to hoard God's promises and blessings for herself and for her son. She wants to do away with the outsiders,

Hagar and Ishmael, so Sarah's side of the family tree can reign supreme, secure in the knowledge that they alone are truly God's favorites. We're still struggling to accept the fact that God loves and cares for both sides of the family tree. We're still struggling with the notion that God cares not just for us, but for all those we would prefer to cast out and keep at a distance—whether they are desperate, homeless single mothers, for whom Hagar is the Bible's first representative, or whether they are Muslims.

As followers of Jesus Christ, we follow a different way, and our calling is to show the way of Jesus Christ to the world. There is no more urgent task for us in the twenty-first century than to figure out how we are going to live at peace and share our ever shrinking world with our brothers and sisters who call God by a different name. God made it clear four thousand years ago that casting them out was not God's plan.

The Genesis account of Abraham, Sarah, Hagar and Ishmael tells us that Jews, Christians, and Muslims all came from the same family. We share a spiritual ancestor, Abraham. We share many of the same sacred stories, although we sometimes interpret them differently. We share the same God, who has promised to bless us all, to make us great, and to be our God, forever and ever, world without end. In the desert, God opened Hagar's eyes, enabling her to see a well of life giving water. She and Ishmael drank deeply. The water saved their lives.

Notice that Ishmael was Abraham's son, but he was rejected and kicked out of the family into being a slave and a servant. Ishmael means "God Hears." He is out in the desert abandoned by his father. He no longer has a daddy. He now feels like an orphan all his life. His life is in a state of conflict. In the middle, there is Hagar who is crying out because she sees Ishmael in desperation. And there is a well that has water available. Ishmael represents the more than one billion Muslims of the Islam nations, one billion Hindus, 600,000 Buddhist, atheist, etc.—all in conflict.[31]

Ministers like Leif Hetland and Global Mission Awareness have seen in the 10/40 parallel a Father hunger as not seen before. Thousands have converted to Christianity. They are craving the love of a Father and his affirmation that "You are my son and daughter with whom I am well pleased." They are living their lives as orphans and are crying out to re-establish an intimate relationship with the Father.

MOSES
The next Biblical account of the orphan heart occurs in the story of Moses. In the written sermon, "Moses as Orphan to Sonship," the Reverend Harold Martin discusses God's healing transformation of Moses from one into the other.

One of the Bible's classic examples of an orphan heart is Moses.

History of the Hebrews prior to Moses

The story starts out with Jacob whose name was changed to Israel after an all night wrestling match with the angel of the Lord. Jacob was the son of Isaac and Rebecca, the grandson of Abraham and Sarah and of Bethuel, and the twin brother of Esau. He had twelve sons and one daughter. Joseph was his Father's favorite son. Joseph was separated from his father Jacob at the age of 17 when his brothers, who had been jealous of his dreams of kingship over them, sold him to traders heading down to Egypt. Jacob was deeply grieved by the loss of his favorite son, and refused to be comforted. Unbeknown to the family, Joseph was sold as a slave to Potiphar, Pharaoh's chief butcher. Joseph resisted the advances of his master's wife for a long time. Finally she accosted him and then accused him of trying to rape her. Even though Joseph was trying to do the right thing, he was thrown into prison.

After Joseph had spent twelve years in prison, the Pharaoh of Egypt had two troubling dreams. His butler recalled having met Joseph in the prison and that he was a successful interpreter of dreams. Joseph is called from prison and interprets the dreams prophesying seven years of abundance followed by seven years of famine. Pharaoh was so impressed that he made Joseph viceroy (second in command)

During the time Joseph was viceroy of the entire Egyptian empire, the famine becomes very severe in Egypt and Canaan. Through a series of events, Joseph reveals his true identity to his brothers and has Jacob resettle the entire family in Egypt. They are given the Land of Goshen by the Pharaoh. The Bible tells us Joseph's brothers thought they had sold him into slavery, but God had turned what they intended for harm into something very good. God used that act of jealously and rebellion to pave the way to preserve the prosperity of Israel. The pharaoh showed great favor to the Hebrews. He gave them the choicest land in all of Egypt. They prospered, owned land, and had their own houses. They enjoyed favor from pharaoh and from the people of Egypt.

Sometime later, Joseph, his brothers, and the entire generation that had moved to Egypt, died. However, the Israelites were fruitful and prolific. They became so numerous and strong that the land was filled with them. Then a new King, who knew nothing of Joseph or the God of Joseph, came to power in Egypt. With a change in leadership came a change in attitude towards the Hebrews. He said to his subjects, "Look how numerous and powerful the Israelite people are growing, more so than we ourselves! Let us stop their increase; otherwise, in time of war they too may join our enemies to fight against us." Their plot was to deal shrewdly with the Hebrews. They would oppress them and then treat them ruthlessly.

They first devised a plan to get the Hebrews to leave Goshen. They deceived the Hebrews into moving to the cities of Pithom and Rameses to help build fortresses and storehouses for pharaoh. Once they left Goshen, their houses and land were confiscated by the Egyptian leaders. Slowly the Hebrew workers became slave laborers and were forced to work under the oppression of the pharaoh.

The word "oppress" means to subject people to harsh or cruel domination, to stress or trouble someone, to browbeat, subjugate, demoralize, or exploit. They were dealt with shrewdly and were now being treated ruthlessly. The Egyptians were slowly and progressively taking away what the previous pharaoh had given to them. They were losing their homes, their land, their freedom, and all the rights and privileges that they had enjoyed. They were being forced into slave labor, degraded, and demoralized. All honor, acceptance, and approval was being stripped away. They were becoming a stench in the nostrils of the Egyptians. (This sounds much like the plight of the church in America today—we are slowly becoming the bad guys—a stench in the nostrils of society). Slavery was the culture of the Hebrews prior to the birth of Moses.

We know that wounding in a person's life can start as early as in the womb. The feelings, emotions, and the response to life's experiences that the mother has can be translated to her unborn baby. The problem is that they are not always properly interpreted by the child.

What would being in that culture say to a Hebrew baby in the womb? Life is too hard, the outside world is not safe, there is no one to look out for you, and no one to protect you. To survive outside the womb you must be independent and self-reliant. You cannot trust anyone. All of this would lay the foundation for an orphan heart in the mind of a child while still in the womb.

Next in pharaoh's plan was to eliminate the Hebrews. Pharaoh commanded the midwives to kill all the male Hebrew babies. The Egyptian midwives feared the God of Hebrews so they found a way around that order. When he discovered that male babies were not being killed, he commanded that all boys that were born were to be thrown into the Nile River.

The Birth of Moses

It was during this time that Miriam, Moses sister, prophesied that a son born to her parents, Amram and Jochedbed, would be the deliverer of Israel from the oppression of pharaoh. It was in this environment that Moses was conceived. We may not always understand the timing of the Lord, but we can rest assured it is always perfect for his plan.

However, in this environment a mom does not want to be pregnant. Dad does not want mom pregnant. They may have wanted a child desperately, but not under these circumstances.

The things being imparted to Moses are fear, a lack of security, and a lack of value or purpose. None of the basic emotional needs of life are being imparted to Moses while he is in the womb.

The lie he believes is that you have to look out for yourself. You must prove yourself by what you can do. You have no value. The best thing you can do is run and hide from life and all of its responsibilities. All of these are components of an orphan heart.

After Moses was born, he was hidden for three months. Hiding, for whatever reason, opens the door to darkness.

This produces more fears. There is the fear of man, the fear of exposure, the fear about what and who you are. There would be feelings of worthlessness, having no value. There would be feelings of shame because you cannot be brought out to life or because you are not welcomed to life. How many people today have complained to God about things like that? You are not happy with you. You felt God could have done a better job than he did, placed you in a better situation or environment than he did. How many sons and daughters have become orphans and taken on an orphan heart because of the circumstances or situation they were born into?

When Moses' mother could no longer hide him, she placed him in a basket and placed him in the Nile. We know the story, we know why it was done, and we can easily see this as an act of tremendous love and sacrifice. To Moses it was abandonment, isolation, no one cares for me, and there is no one to look after me.

Moses was recovered by people he didn't know, taken to a strange environment, and surrounded by people and things that he was not familiar with.

It is good that Moses' sister suggested to the pharaoh's daughter about getting someone to nurse him, and his mother is brought in to nurse him. It was probably during this time that the destiny of Moses was imparted to him. But, she is not a mom to Moses. Instead, she is the nurse that feeds him. Then when Moses is weaned, she is taken away. His only connection to his world is removed. Moses experiences more isolation and more abandonment. More of the orphan heart is imparted to Moses.

Moses was raised by a father he did not know, in an environment he did not belong. Moses knows something is different about him because he looks different, he acts different, and his desires are different.

You were created on purpose, with a purpose, and for a purpose.

Before I formed you in the womb I knew you, before you were born I set you apart *(Acts 17:26)*.

God determined the time you should be born and the places you should live *(Jeremiah 1:5)*.

Your purpose, your destiny, and the desire of God for you are set in your heart from the time you are born. John 1:3 tells us, "God's seed remains in us." That seed, the DNA of God, is always calling us towards our destiny. The problem comes when wounding distorts our vision, our understanding, and imparts orphan mentality into our hearts. Now it is harvest time for the seeds that were planted in Moses.

One day Moses goes out to visit his people. He sees an Egyptian abusing a fellow Hebrew and kills the Egyptian. An orphan heart makes a murderer and a fugitive out of Moses. Moses flees to Midian and ends up in the house of Jethro/Reuel—the priest of Midian. Zipporah, the daughter of Jethro, becomes the wife of Moses and they have two sons.

Moses has spent 40 years in Egypt developing the heart of a leader. He now spends 40 years on the back side of the desert developing the heart of a shepherd. None of that time was wasted. God can turn all our seemingly wasted years into times of preparation for his service. God can take the broken and make more than a master piece. He can make a miracle. The greatest of all miracles is transforming the heart of an orphan into the heart of a son. For Moses that transformation begins with his encounter with God at the burning bush.

A major characteristic of the orphan heart is the lack of trust. Because of the lack of trust there is an abundance of distrust. In other words, nothing or nobody is ever what it appears to be. The heart is closed and the mind is very skeptical. Dr. Grant Mullen has stated that where there is a lack of trust, especially trust in God, fear will always come to replace it. An orphan heart is filled with all types of fears.

One day while looking for lost sheep, Moses sees a very strange sight. He sees a bush that is burning with fire but is not being consumed. Moses turned aside to investigate.

Once God had Moses' attention, he could begin to transform his heart. God said, "Take off your shoes." Why? Moses is out in the desert. He is not at the temple. He is on the side of a mountain listening to a talking bush that is burning with fire but not being consumed.

Take off your shoes. The place you are standing is holy. God is saying: Moses, you are special. You stand in a special place with me. One of the deficits in the heart of an orphan is value. God begins the transformation of the orphan heart of Moses by imparting value to Moses.

Take off your shoes. It is a simple act that says a lot. In many of the eastern cultures today you take off your shoes when you enter the home. Taking off your shoes demonstrates that you belong there. In America we may say something like, "Make yourself at home." It is something that imparts value to others and makes them feel like they belong. A person with an orphan heart needs to feel like they belong.

Take off your shoes. God is also saying to Moses: Let's begin to remove what separates you from intimacy with me. God wants nothing of this world to come between you and him. God is telling Moses to step out of what you are and step into what He has called you to be. Step out of being an orphan and step into being a son. Step out of your past and step into the future I have for you. In Moses' eyes and in his heart he was a great failure. He was a murderer and a fugitive. He was a man without a real home. God is beginning to displace all of those feelings by imparting value, significance, and worth to Moses. He is telling Moses: you stand in a special place with me. That is the same message every person with an orphan heart needs to hear. You are special to the Father, the Father himself loves you, and you have a home in him.

From value God now moves to establishing trust and credibility with Moses. He meets Moses where he is so he can take him where he needs to go. As God establishes trust and credibility with Moses, he then moves towards something vital to displacing the heart of an orphan by imparting purpose.

God is saying: I am so concerned about my people that I am sending you, Moses. I am going to rescue them and I am going to do it through you. This declaration of trust, value, and confidence is overwhelming for Moses.

His orphan heart rises up in opposition. I can't do this. You have made a mistake. You got the wrong guy. I am a bad choice, God. Get someone else. Next, God applies a very vital technique for displacing the orphan heart— persistence. Persistence is the only thing that will over-come resistance.

God tells Moses exactly what he is to do and exactly what will happen when he does it. He is telling Moses the end from the beginning, so that Moses will learn that he can trust God every step of the way. He is teaching Moses His ways before he shows Israel his deeds.

This whole process shows us how hard it is to displace the orphan heart. Over the years and through all the experiences that have confirmed wrong beliefs, we see how deeply orphan mentality can run.

As Moses is listening to all God is saying, his orphan heart responds with fear. One of fear's greatest defense weapons is the "what if." If the enemy can get you going down the "what if" road, he knows he can sidetrack your destiny. Moses declares "what if" and God responds with demonstrations of power. The demonstrations of power were to show Moses the "what if" did not matter. No weapon formed against you will prevail: no plan, no scheme, and no insight that can succeed against the Lord.

Remember God's response to Paul's pleas about the thorn—which was demonic attacks assigned against Paul: *My grace is sufficient for you, for my power is made perfect in weakness* (2 Corinthians 12:9).

In Exodus 4:10 in the Amplified Bible, Moses said to the lord, *"O Lord, I am not eloquent or a man of words, neither before nor since you have spoken to your servant; for I am slow of speech and have a heavy and awkward tongue."* It appears that at some point in time Moses overcame this obstacle. In Acts 7:22, Stephen declared that Moses was educated in all the wisdom of the Egyptians and was powerful in speech and action. As we move out of orphan mentality and into sonship, God will change even our physical handicaps and limitations into assets. God can use what we see as a defect or deficiency to open doors to the hearts of people no one else could ever minister to.

Due to all of Moses' resistance to the call of God, the anger of the Lord burned against him. The denial of your destiny will irritate God. The final plea of the orphan heart is I can't do it. I know you have called me. I know you have equipped me. I know you will go with me. I know I am out of excuses but, God, I just don't feel like I can do it.

As you follow the story of the Exodus you see how God was with Moses every step of the way. When it appeared that what they were doing was not working, when the situation appeared to be getting worst, God encouraged

Moses. He told Moses: Now you will see what I am going to do to pharaoh. We see Moses' heart change from timid and doubtful to confident and powerful. Moses was indeed being moved from a man with an orphan heart to a man who walked in sonship.

One of the greatest points in the process was when they came to the Red Sea. The Egyptians are closing in. The Hebrews are crying out, "Why did you bring us out of Egypt"? Moses cries out to God. God responds, "Why are you crying out to me?" God was not abandoning Moses. It was a father's declaration of total confidence in his son. Moses obeys the word of the Lord, and we see one of the greatest miracles recorded in history. The Red Sea is parted. The Hebrews walk through it on dry land. The Egyptians pursue them and the entire army is drowned.

God continues to confirm Moses. He provides water out of a rock when they were thirsty. He provides quail and manna when they were hungry.

I believe we can see the process of displacing the orphan heart with a heart of sonship completed after the incident of the golden calf. We see Moses confronting God on behalf of the Hebrews. God changes His mind about destroying them and says He will continue with them. After that Moses—now acting like a man who understood his position as a son; asking God to show him His glory. Asking to see the glory of God is like asking to see all that makes God who He is. Moses is saying: Show me all that there is to know about You. I want to know You personally and intimately. That is the heart of a son wanting to know the heart of his father.

From that point on you see God contending with those that contended with Moses. He blessed all that Moses did. He brought honor and favor to Moses. Moses begins to live in the blessings of sonship.[32]

MARTHA OR MARY
Martha tries to show Jesus how much she loves him but instead her orphan heart gets in the way of intimacy.

Working Hard to Please Jesus
or Just Spending Time with Him

As Jesus and his disciples were on their way *(remember that Jesus is on his way to Jerusalem to DIE)*, he came to a village where a woman named Martha opened her home to him. She had a sister called Mary, who sat at the Lord's feet listening to what he said. But Martha was distracted by all the preparations that had to be made. She came to him and asked, "Lord, don't you care that my sister has left me to do the work by myself? Tell her to help me!" "Martha, Martha," the Lord answered, "You are worried and upset about many things, but only one thing is needed Mary has chosen what is better, and it will not be taken away from her." *(Luke 10:38-42)*.

Jesus is visiting the house of Martha and her sister Mary. Martha busies herself with preparations for the meal, while Mary sits at Jesus' feet listening to him. Martha was eager to celebrate Jesus' visit by putting out the best that the house could offer. I would bet that some of you have an aunt that is just like that. Jesus loved Martha and Martha loved him, but when she set out to be kind, it had to be her way of being kind. This is one characteristic of an orphan heart. When Martha complains that she could do with a little help, Jesus tells her that Mary is doing the better thing: it is better to spend time with Jesus than to be busy with too much work. This is the classic story of how people become too busy doing good works to please God instead of just spending time with Him, sitting in His lap, and experiencing His love flowing out over us. Have you ever had a time in your life when you were sitting with someone else and not having a conversation. Conversation was not needed. It is all about relationship. Mary understood this. Jesus says: only one thing is needed. All he wanted was to spend time in an intimate relationship with them.[33]

THE PRODIGAL SON

This is the classic story of the prodigal son, which has been told from hundreds of different points of view. It is about the orphan heart, about inheritance, about adoption, about obeying the father, about relationship with the father, about the second son, about becoming a slave, about sonship, about unconditional love, about the third son who is telling the story, and finally about the love of the Father's heart.

Here we have a story about a son that is living in his father's house where he receives love, is affirmed as lovable by his father, is part of a family unit, has a secure place to sleep in, and has a sense of belonging.

And He said, "A man had two sons. The younger of them said to his father, 'Father, give me the share of the estate that falls to me.' *(inheritance)* So he divided his wealth between them." *(Luke 15:11).*

According to William Barkley in his commentary on the Gospel of Luke:

Under Jewish law, a father was not able to distribute his property, as he liked. It was not unusual for a father to distribute his estate before he died. The elder son must get two thirds and the younger one third (cf., Deuteronomy 21:17).[34]

However, Jack Frost points out that:

> In the culture of that day...the father was in no way required to give his son an early inheritance, and in fact, according to Jewish law of that day, the father could have given his son a stoning as punishment for dishonoring his father.[35]

This younger son was essentially saying, "Dad, I wish you were dead.... I can't wait for you to die. Give me what is rightfully mine so that I can leave home and get on with life!" The father knew that if the son was ever to learn, he must learn through tough love. Therefore, he granted the request. The son turned away from the father, left him, and became an orphan.

> In the midst of the father's humiliation, brokenness, and pain, the father is not only compassionate, but also extremely generous. He gave his son the inheritance without anger or judgment, despite the son's greed and selfishness.... He allows his younger son's portion of the estate (about one third) to be sold so that his son can receive the funds. He has already forgiven his son for his rebellion, or he would have never have given him the inheritance.[36]
>
> Jesus wanted to teach a lesson about the restoration of a relationship with God that had already existed; a homecoming to a Father's love after the bond of intimacy had been broken by our immaturity.[37]

And not many days later, the younger son gathered everything together and went on a journey into a distant country, and there he squandered his estate with loose living. *(Sonship into orphan heart living—wine, women, and song.)* Now when he had spent everything, a severe famine occurred in that country, and he began to be impoverished. *(Luke 15:13).*

When we cease abiding in God's love and begin drifting away from an intimate relationship with Him, it is time to heed the still, small voice within: "Warning! You are about to hurt the people around you! Warning! Warning!" Looking for intimacy that had been so prevalent in Father's house, we may seek to replace it with a false sense of intimacy derived from pornography, addictions, compulsions, or sexual immorality[38]

So he went and hired himself out to one of the citizens of that country, and he sent him into his fields to feed swine. *(Luke 15:15).*

For a Jew, this work was lower than that given to the slaves. It was also forbidden to a Jew because the law said, "Cursed is he who feeds swine."

And he would have gladly filled his stomach with the pods that the swine were eating, and no one was giving anything to him. But when he came to his senses, he said, 'How many of my father's hired men have more than enough bread, but I am dying here with hunger!' *(Luke 15:16-17).*

Even the slaves were in some sense a member of the family unit. It was only the hired day laborers or servants that could be dismissed at a day's notice.

The Love of the Father's Heart
Unconditional Love

"I will get up and go to my father, and will say to him, 'Father, I have sinned against heaven, and in your sight; I am no longer worthy to be called your son; make me as one of your hired men.' So he got up and came to his father. But while he was still a long way off, his father saw him and felt compassion for him, and ran and embraced him and kissed him." *(Luke 15:18-20).*

The father had already forgiven his son before he left home. The love he had for his son was not based on his behavior. He was simply waiting for his son to return so that he could fully express his affectionate love. This is the same love that orphans are denied when they have an absentee father in their life. This is the same love that orphan adults subconsciously seek in their life to fill that void of Father hunger. Some believe that the father so loved his son and missed him so much, that every morning he would go out to a place from where he could see a far distance and look for his son. "Many, many times this father has looked down that road, waiting for his younger son's return. Seeing a figure in the distance, he has said, "Perhaps this is him. Perhaps this is my son." Then, as the figure has come closer, he has recognized the form and with disappointment in his voice said, "No, it's just one of my hired men coming in from the field."

But finally, the day arrives—the day of the joyous homecoming! There in the distance, his head hanging down, defeated and ashamed, is his youngest son. The father recognizes him at once and he runs. Yes, he RUNS to meet him.

The incredible thing about this story is that Jesus is really talking about His own Father and He's picturing Him as a man who RUNS to meet His son. As far as I know, it's the only place in Scripture where we see God running.[39]

> And the son said to him, "Father, I have sinned against heaven and in your sight; I am no longer worthy to be called your son." (*Luke 15:21*).

The son never got a chance to ask his father to receive him back as like his lowest hired servant. The father receives him back as his son in a relationship of sonship.

But the father said to his slaves, "Quickly bring out the best robe and put it on him, and put a ring on his hand and sandals on his feet." *(Luke 15:22).*

This is the unconditional love of the father's heart. Remember that he ran, embraced him, and kissed him. He did not say, "Oh my God, what is that horrendous smell?" Remember that his son has been living with the pigs amongst all the pig manure. He must have smelled worse than a cesspool. And then he said, "Quickly, bring out a robe and put it on him." He could have said, "Go bathe yourself before you put on my robe." The robe was the father's best robe and stood for honor, and the ring of inheritance, for authority. His father's unconditional love accepted his son back into the family just the way he was. He did not wait for an apology to make sure his son was sincere.

Our Heavenly Father, the One who is depicted in the parable, is just like that. He doesn't keep his distance. He does not wait for an apology. He does not outline conditions for his son's return. Instead, filled with compassion, He RUNS, arms open wide, to receive him.[40]

"And bring the fattened calf, kill it, and let us eat and celebrate; for this son of mine was dead and has come to life again; he was lost and has been found."And they began to celebrate *(Luke 15:23-24).*

He rejoiced that his long lost, beloved son had returned. This is an example of Father God's love and forgiveness for his sons and daughters.

The Older Son

Now his older son was in the field, and when he came and approached the house, he heard music and dancing. And he summoned one of the servants and began inquiring what these things could be. And he said to him, "Your brother has come, and your father has killed the fattened calf because he has received him back safe and sound." But he became angry and was not willing to go in; and his father came out and began pleading with him. But he answered and said to his father, "Look! For so many years I have been serving you and I have never neglected a command of yours; and yet you have never given me a young goat, so that I might celebrate with my friends; but when this son of yours came, who has devoured your wealth with prostitutes, you killed the fattened calf for him." And he said to him, "Son, you have always been with me, and all that is mine is yours. But we had to celebrate and rejoice, for this brother of yours was dead and has begun to live, and was lost and has been found." *(Luke 15:25-32)*.

Notice that the older son is saying how hard he has worked for the father, obeying his father's laws and commands, doing all the right things, but never receiving any rewards for it. As soon as the older brother drifts away from the father's house because of a negative attitude of self love, jealousy, or fundamentalism, an emotional and spiritual distance is immediately created between him and his father. Any distance from God's love will gradually gravitate to law and legalism, and it will lead to feelings of insecurity, because it is the unconditional acceptance of the Father that gives us our true value and self worth.[41] He doesn't even acknowledge that his brother has come back home. He refers to him as "this son of yours." He has lack of sympathy toward his brother through his self righteous character. Again, we see the father's forgiveness when he tells his oldest son that he has always been loved as a son, even if they did not celebrate his sonship. All that is mine is yours. You have always been part of my family. But your brother left the family and was dead. And now he is back again as my son. So, we had to celebrate and rejoice.

The father pleads with him to come and join the party. But the older son is angry. In fact, his anger, having festered over time, has become a root of bitterness. After all, this young man, this brother of his, is breaking his father's heart.

Yes, the older son knows all about it. Stories of immorality, wild parties, and riotous living have brought shame to him and his family. Even in a distant country, news travels fast.

But this isn't the worst of it. If only his father would stop grieving. But day after day, without fail, he stands at the door, looking down that dusty road for the younger son's return—longing for him, waiting for him, praying for him. Why would he want this younger son, this brother of his, to come home?

No. He will not go in! This younger brother deserves to be punished. He has broken the bank. He has broken the Law. What the older son does not realize is that even as he judges his younger brother, he is bringing that same judgment back upon himself.

"Be merciful, just as your Father is merciful. Do not judge, and you will not be judged. Do not condemn, and you will not be condemned. Forgive, and you will be forgiven." *(Luke 6:36-37)*

The younger son embraces the spirit of the world and becomes captive to his own lustful desires, while the older son embraces the spirit of religion and becomes captive to his own pride and self righteousness.[42]

Are we not like the older son? Are we allowing the traditions of men to ensnare us in the complex of legalism? We are if we rely on our good works as a means to salvation or spiritual growth. We are if we insist that others follow a certain list of rules to be accepted within our Christian community.

God is not interested in our good works or our rules. There is nothing we can do, nothing we can offer Him as a Holy God that He can accept—except our faith in Jesus Christ.

Has someone told us that we need to be baptized, join the church, take Holy Communion, teach a Sunday school class, feed the poor, or donate large sums of money to religious charities to inherit eternal life?

This is legalism. Nowhere in the Word of God does it tell us we have to do any of these things.

Salvation is by the grace of God through faith. Grace is God doing for us what we can't do for ourselves. It has nothing to do with good works.

Has someone told us that if we want to mature in Christ we need to read our Bibles, fast, pray, win souls, memorize Scripture, attend church faithfully, and tithe?

This, too, is legalism. When someone tries to give us a list of rules or guidelines in terms of how many hours we should spend in Bible study and prayer, how many verses of Scripture we should memorize, or how many souls we should win for Christ, beware!

Has someone told us we must give up alcohol, tobacco, movies, dancing, playing cards, popular music, comic books, or certain types of food if we want to be accepted as a church member in good standing? Or as women that we are never to wear slacks, sleeveless blouses, makeup, short hair, or skirts that are at least one inch below the knee.

This too, is legalism. When we try to create an arbitrary standard for Christian conduct, we are misusing the Word of God. We are placing the focus on ourselves, what we do or don't do, instead of on the Lord Jesus Christ![43]

Symptoms of the Older Brother Syndrome

Shiloh Place Ministries in its Experiencing Father's Embrace School identifies the symptoms of older brother's jealousy.

> Any theology, duty, or service that is not rooted and grounded in the unconditional love of God can gradually gravitate towards law and legalism.

1. Aggressive striving and hyper-religious activity.

The harder the older brother slaved in the fields trying to earn his father's blessing, the more distant he grew from the love he sought. The more addicted you become to trying to earn acceptance through aggressive striving, the more of an angry edge develop towards those who do not agree with your way of thinking.

2. Sibling rivalry and competing for acceptance and affirmation.

Once you begin to strive for love and acceptance, you easily take on an "us" versus "them" mentality—those who think and believe like me against those who do not; those who are for me, can promote, or can profit me against those who are not of value for me. We seem to believe that if we can only "succeed" and be up front in a place where people see us and bless us more and we will feel more loved and accepted. This often leads to sibling rivalry and envy—feelings of ill will for those in the same line of work. When we have a need for some spiritual achievement or distinction, and have a willingness to strive to attain it (spiritual ambition), then we begin to believe we are not honored or blessed if we are the center of attention. This reveals we have drifted off-center of Father's love and are in need of a homecoming.

3. Feeling that you are not favored leads to resentments.

When we work hard to be loved, we begin comparing ourselves to others. It can lead to frustrations over feelings that we do not match up, which can become resentment. Feeling more like a devoted servant than a favored son or daughter increases the possibility of resentment towards those who seem more blessed than you. You are no longer able to rejoice when others are blessed. You may even begin to delight when others fall or their weaknesses are exposed. Our unconscious anger at not feeling value or love can lead to a lifestyle of resentments because we have felt that life has not been fair. Youthful hidden core pain plus aggressive striving can equal an angry edge to our ministry, our service, or our home life.

4. Resentments eventually lead to a critical and judgmental attitude.

A person with a critical spirit is often angry because he feels as if he has not been given the love and honor he was created to receive. He may feel life has not been fair and others have not worked as hard—others are not as holy, others are not as disciplined, others are not as theologically correct. There is no love in law and legalism.

Finding Our Way Home to Father's Embrace

The transition from living by the love of the law to embracing the law of love requires a repositioning of our heart and attitudes. Here are some simple keys to coming home to Father's embrace.

1. Acknowledge the symptoms of the older brother syndrome in our lives.

2. We need to experience movement towards a life-style of confession and repentance of each misrepresentation of Father's love and grace.
3. We need movement towards the ministry of restitution.
4. We need movement towards experiencing Father's love and affirmation.[44]

This concludes our survey of the origins of the orphan heart. I don't think it is an accident that so many of the early Biblical accounts deal with that heart-rending condition. Obviously, it has troubled human beings throughout history, although it has never been as pervasive as it is in our times.

Next, we will look at the characteristics of people who suffer with an orphan heart.

Chapter Two
The Orphan Heart Attitude

In researching the literature available on an orphan heart, I realized that every resource would have the reader believe that all orphans develop an orphan heart mental attitude during childhood development. Then I realized that it is not justified to lump all orphans into a category and then decide that all of them would have the same characteristics. If we interview several people born in June, such as me, and conclude that these people are introverted, shy, creative, late bloomers, etc., then we would be amiss if we assumed that all people born in June have these same characteristics. It may fit the majority but not the total group. Therefore, assuming that all fatherless children have characteristics of an orphan heart attitude would not be correct either. Only a portion of the sample group would experience these attitudes.

An orphan heart is a mental attitude developed from external stimuli (experiences) during child development and influenced by parental nurturing and emotional presence in the child's life. An orphan heart feels that it does not have a safe and secure place in a father's heart, where it is loved, valued, and affirmed. It is the same as if we experience love from our heart or that our heart feels lonely, unloved, hurt, happy, and sad, etc. Biologically our heart does not feel these emotions but our brain thinks so. Therefore, if our heart feels that we are an orphan with orphan characteristics, then our brain thinks in terms of an orphan or what is called orphan thinking. My heart feels that I am not lovable, and therefore I think I am not lovable. My orphan thinking then leads me to think that God doesn't love me because I am not lovable. In addition, what my mind believes controls my actions, emotions, and personality traits. What I believe to be true is true to me even if it is a lie. Orphan heart thinking leads to orphan heart living.

At Shiloh Place Ministries, the orphan heart is defined as "someone who does not feel they have a safe place of value in the heart of a loving father." Out of this lack, many people deal with feelings of abandonment. Now, of course we can reason the feelings of abandonment away in knowing that our fathers were doing a good thing, as in the case of the World War II veterans, but I believe if you have the fruit of it in your life somewhere, then what is the root of this?

> Getting saved does not break the orphan life. The only way to break the orphan life is to introduce it to a father and when it is loved by a father, it is an orphan no more. That is why the revelation of the Father is so important. Being born again removes our sins from us and brings us into the kingdom—but it does not mean we know the Father unless we are fathered—until He becomes a Father to us.[45]

My dad was killed in World War II before I was born and my mother never remarried. Therefore, I didn't have my dad around to affirm that I was like him, that I was lovable, and that he loved me. I didn't have strong male images in my life to teach me what it meant to be a male child. My grandfather was a strong willed Polish immigrant, who ruled over his house of 10 kids with an iron hand. Even though I loved my grandfather dearly, I always had an intense fear of him and the day that I would do something to make him very mad. Unfortunately, that day came as my grandparents watched over me while Mom went out of town. I hid in the barn where grandpa couldn't find me until my mom came to get me. How was I to know that grandpa's kittens couldn't swim on top of the water in the rain barrel?

My aunts have repeatedly told me how much my mother loved me when I was a child even after she received the telegram in April of 1945 that Dad was killed in action. I don't remember my mother being a hugging and loving person that affirmed that I was lovable and that she loved me. In my mind, our relationship is what I will call the Karen Carpenter parents syndrome (from the movie), where the parents feel no need to tell the children how much they are loved because they just know. They don't need to be hugged and kissed as part of that love. The parents were always emotionally detached and distant. Maybe your parents were like that. Maybe you came from a country that has a cold culture.

> Rejection can even be felt by children of well meaning parents who fail to hug, touch or express affection. This creates an environment of emotional neglect. When a sibling dies or parents separate, a vulnerable child may feel rejected by the departing family member and may even

feel responsible for the loss, which then triggers self rejection. Children who have never met their father or who were abandoned by him suffer from a very deep wound of rejection. All forms of abuse are types of rejections.[46]

I always knew I was different in some ways from other kids. I never wanted to socialize. I just wanted to be left alone in a corner all by myself. Probably because I didn't have my dad around to play with me. I did well playing in a corner of a sand box by myself while the other kids played on the opposite side. From what I remember, I was always doing things for my mother that ended up proving myself to be worthy somehow. I remember being fascinated with pianos and music at an early age. I loved going to the neighbors because they had an old player piano, which played music from rolls of paper. Later on, I took dance and ballet lessons, for what purpose no one can tell me why to this day. It wasn't my decision. Mom would push me to be the best. One time, when I refused to practice my dance steps, she locked me in our dark basement until I did. I knew in my head she loved me and that she did this out of that love, but it left a permanent wound in my soul, which reinforced the orphan heart of being not loved and unlovable. I later became part of a dancing duet at the age of seven, and a star of the dance school performing on stage at the Stanley Theater. Thus began the part of my life when I became a perfectionist and overachiever to prove that I was lovable and worthy of love. I was loved. Listen to the applause. Take a bow.

It was 1950 when we moved to New Hartford, New York. I think it was also that year that Mom developed breast cancer and started her fight for life. During the next five years she wasn't around much. Most of the time, she was in and out of hospitals undergoing surgeries or treatments that made her ill. I was cared for by my grandmother and my aunts. My grandmother taught me how to crochet and hold balls of yarn for her knitting. Learning how to play sports and do guy things just wasn't part of my childhood. By the age of seven or eight, I was able to take a city bus to go to the YMCA for swimming classes and general swim. I didn't fit in well, and the other kids didn't seem to like me much. By now, I was a little man in a kid's birthday suit. I was getting used to being a rejected unlovable person. I felt that I must become perfect. I must prove to everybody in the world that I am worthy to be loved and justified to be a person.

Then in 1955, my mother sat me down in grandma's living room and told me that I must decide where I want to go live if she should die. I screamed and screamed that I didn't want to go anywhere, but Mom said I must choose. I decided on Aunt Helen and Uncle Stan, who wanted me–I would live with them. However, my mother said I couldn't and gave me several reasons why not. I then said I would go to live with my cousins in Detroit, but my mom said that that was not an option either. The one place I did not want to go and live was the only option my mother gave me.

Before October 7 of that year, I was taken to the hospital to visit my mom. The scene in the movie "Terms of Endearment" where the children are taken into the hospital room to see their dying mom for the last time still tears me up. That is what happened to me. That was the last time I saw her alive. She gave me a hug, and then she gave me a curse. She said, "Go live with your aunt and uncle, be a big boy, be a good boy, study hard, and become a doctor." It took 53 years before I was able to grieve my mother's death. At the funeral, I shed no tears and I made up my mind that from that time on I would feel nothing. I had been betrayed and abandoned. There was no one left I could trust and no one to love me. My safe and secure home was ripped out from under my feet. I had begun to develop an orphan heart/orphan spirit.

An orphan's heart rejects parental authority, seeks control to do everything "my way," never feels truly at home anywhere, is afraid to trust, is afraid of rejection, is afraid to receive love, is afraid of intimacy, and cannot unconditionally express love.

According to Jack Frost in his book "Spiritual Slavery to Spiritual Sonship," all of us are:

> ...born with an orphan heart that...seeks independence...rejects parental authority."[47]

When you possess an orphan heart, you never truly feel at home anywhere. You are afraid to trust, afraid of rejection, and afraid to open up your heart to receive love. And unless you are able to receive love, you cannot unconditionally express love, even to your own family. It has taken me years to discover the truth. My research continually opens my eyes to a deeper understanding of the orphan heart. It is so important in the world we now live in to understand how we are orphans and how we got there. My orphan heart never truly allowed me to feel at home living with my aunt, uncle, and cousin. I was afraid to trust, afraid of rejection, and afraid to receive love. Remember, that at my mother's funeral I made an inner vow that I would never allow myself to feel again. I totally closed my heart to receive love. Without being able to receive love, I could not unconditionally express love to anyone. I was being shuffled off to YMCA and Boy Scout summer camps, and I never could understand why. It wasn't my decision to go to summer camp. I figured that if they didn't want me around, I would make my own plans. I started reading magazines about military schools. Then I devised my master plan to run away to

California. I figured I could ride my bike 20 miles a days. I collected all kinds of maps and charted out the route I would take. However, something stopped me from going. Instead, I started planning for the day when I would be free to leave. It would be only eight years. I would go to college far, far away. I would enjoy life. I would become the prodigal son.

I suppose that if you look at the other side of the story, my aunt and uncle were doing everything they could think of to help me become a better person. I just wouldn't let them.

My uncles all tried their best to be substitute fathers in my life. They took me fishing but never showed me how to fish or bait a hook. I guess that I was supposed to just know about that on my own. I hated those squishy worms that I couldn't get on the hook when I stabbed at them on a rock. I never got the fishing line into the water before it was time to go home. There was no male influence or instruction in my life during this phase of being a boy. I was taken for little league tryouts after days of practicing with a baseball. The instructor sent a bunch of us out to the outfield to catch pop flies. When it came to be my turn, he hit the ball, which disappeared into the sun and then landed in the middle of my forehead. I never saw it coming. He said to my uncle, "Maybe next year." My uncle decided to teach me how to caddy for him on Sundays when he played golf. I found that enjoyable and started to become good at it. Then he started to teach me how to play golf. However, the next thing I knew I was entered into a tournament for teenagers that I didn't want to play in. The night before the tournament, we went out to practice on three holes at the golf course. On a long par five, I teed off and sliced the ball so badly that it went straight at some people putting on a nearby green. My uncle was so angry that he took the shaft of his driver and whacked it across my behind, shouting a long list of expletives. I threw my clubs at him. I made up my mind that I would participate in the tournament, but I would never play golf again. The next day I played without caring and turned in a score of 129 for 18 holes. The embarrassment for my uncle was so bad that I was never asked to play golf again. There was no loving father in my life for affirmation. I was at another point of rejection in my life, and not open to love from others. After all, no one really cared about me. My orphan heart was now taking control of my life.

According to Jack Frost:

> Rejection or perceived rejection left unhealed can set into motion in an orphan heart a pathway that eventually manifests as a stronghold of oppression. This is when a deeply entrenched thought structure (mental attitude) becomes a habit that only a profound experience of Father God's love can displace. For those who do not feel they have a safe place of value in the heart of a loving Father have established an orphan heart and therefore may have abandonment issues. The root cause could be because:
>
> 1) You interpret parental faults as disappointment, discouragement, or rejection, which can lead to our own grief.
> 2) Your trust in parental authority is lost. Once disappointed, rejected, or otherwise wounded by a parent, we close off a part of our heart to keep it from being hurt again. A wall goes up. Basic trust is lost.
>
> For some orphans that did not have a father in their childhood:
>
> 3) You develop a fear of receiving love, comfort, and admonition from others. Once basic trust is lost, it becomes

difficult to receive from others because we are afraid to make ourselves vulnerable.

4) You enter into an emotional isolation. I will not allow you to get close to me. I will not allow you to hurt me.

5) You believe that no one cares about you. No one can fulfill your needs.

6) Once we close our hearts to receiving love, we close our hearts to intimacy (in to me see.)[48]

When I had to go and live with my aunt and uncle after my mother's death, I refused to allow them to get close to me and to love me. I made an inner vow that I would never allow myself to get hurt again. I would never allow myself to be emotionally vulnerable again. I did everything I could to make it difficult to be loved, and I refused to allow myself to accept being part of their family. I hated where I was living, and I hated having to live there. I was definitely not going to allow myself to love them.

I firmly believed that my aunt and uncle didn't love me. No one cared about me. I just had to take care of myself.

RELATIONSHIPS AND INTIMACY

If you are uncomfortable with love, you are uncomfortable with yourself. If you are uncomfortable with yourself, you are uncomfortable with others. If you do not believe you are lovable, you may find it difficult to receive God's gift of unmerited love and favor. And it may be difficult to enjoy healthy relationships with others if you view yourself differently from the way God views you.[49]

High school can be one of the most devastating times in a teenager's life especially when it comes to affairs of the heart. Especially for an orphan that has not been well prepared with a solid foundation for love, relationships, and intimacy. I certainly wasn't ready for the life changing experience that came out of nowhere. Here I

was full of an orphan heart attitude with every characteristic operational in my psychological makeup. Then
Lynn sitting next to me in French class became friendly
with me. The next thing I knew, I was walking her home
after school in the complete opposite direction from where
I lived. Soon we were listening to record albums together
after school at her house. We both fell in love with "West
Side Story." I took her to see it at the movie theater, and
from then on I was head over heels in love. Unfortunately,
I allowed myself to be vulnerable for which I paid dearly.
It was about two weeks later when, for some reason, I
became upset that she was late one morning as I went
to meet her getting off the school bus. I said some stupid
things and stormed off. It wasn't her fault that the bus
was late. I realized that I was immature and had done
the wrong thing. Later in the day, I went to talk to her
in the chemistry lab to apologize. I wasn't ready for what
happened next. She unemotionally told me that she didn't
want anything more to do with me and didn't want to see
me again. At that moment, I felt excruciating pain, as if
my heart were being ripped out of my body. I left the lab
and sat down on a desktop in the hallway outside the lab,
barely holding back the tears. I was again rejected and
felt sure that I was unlovable. I swore for the second time
that no one would ever hurt me this way again.

I had no one to turn to. There was no one I could talk
to about this situation—no one in my life that could have
explained to me that this was OK; no one to affirm that
I was loved and lovable; no one to help me work through
the pain of the heartbreak. I was all alone, with no one
to help me but myself. Later that evening, as I sat on my
bedroom floor in tears, I screamed out at God that he
was doing nothing for me in my life and didn't love me.
No one loves me. My aunt and uncle don't love me. Girls
don't love me. Kids in school don't like me. What good are

you? I reject you in my life. Get out. The final stone of the orphan heart had been cemented in place. It marked the beginning of doom and gloom in my life. I became the prodigal son.

In my opinion, some of the best conference speakers and teachers on healing are also the ones who are transparent and open, and allow the public to see the difficult, painful, and traumatic happenings in their life. These would be people like Jack Frost, Leif Hetland, Randy Clark, and Russ Parker. Divulging such previously unknown events leaves one vulnerable and totally exposed.

Jack Frost has written that three things happen when someone is transparent about how God dealt with them and the sins in that person's life. First, a person becomes more sensitive to the shame that a particular sin brings. Confessing to others becomes a catalyst to prevent one from ever committing that sin again. Second, transparent witnessing releases a deeper cleansing and freedom from sins. As long as sins are kept hidden, only confessing them to God, they could easily sneak up again. Third, when someone shares an area of past bondage or habitual sin, other people begin to recognize the sin in their own lives and come under deep personal conviction from that sin.

Reverend Harold Martin states that, "Transparency is the means that releases oneself from bondage that the accuser can use against us. Therefore if everything is known about my life, I hope to accomplish the same."[50]

The importance of a successful adolescent maturation process is explained by Dr. Grant Mullen:

> If our emotional maturation process during puberty pro-cedes correctly, we will pass from a very inward looking, self conscious stage, to an outward looking, self confident stage where we feel secure in our identity and

self worth. To successfully pass through emotional adolescence we must come to the place of self acceptance. To
accomplish this passage, we need to have Godly parents
who themselves have come to emotional maturity so that
they can guide us through these stormy waters.

If a person does not pass through this stage successfully, he will become stuck in the self centered, self conscious, insecure emotional state of adolescence regardless of his biological age. When this happens a person is
unable to accept themselves or to find his own identities.

If development stops at this point, a person will be continually driven by the emotional pain of insecurity, self
consciousness, and inadequacy to search for an identity.
This state is that of being in perpetual emotional adolescence regardless of age.

A person can never find self acceptance in the approval
of others. People caught in this trap will for their whole
lives be introspective, insecure, self critical, anxious and
unsure of themselves.

The shocking reality is that very few of us ever complete this process of self acceptance and release from
emotional adolescence, since we don't have parents,
particularly fathers, who have accepted themselves. An
insecure father is unable to lead his child to self acceptance. This means that many are emotionally fatherless even though their father was present in the home.
*Being fatherless leaves large gaps in our emotional
development and deficiencies in our personalities
where we did not receive enough love or nurture.*
(added emphasis)[51]

Having an absentee father only exacerbates the situation. This could lead to hidden, unconscious wounds in
your soul. A child can feel the absence of a father's love
during childhood development. Its need for a father's love

and affirmation is not being met, which results in emotional depravation.

OUR NEED FOR INTIMACY

Jack Frost of Shiloh Place Ministries in "Seeing the World Experience the Father's Healing Love through the Hearts of the Leaders" writes:

> Many people today (even Christians) do not acknowledge their deep, God given need for intimacy. Intimacy is a willingness to know and be known by others. We are living in a season when God is trying to intimately express His love to us but many do not realize their need for it. "Just let me get saved, filled with the Holy Spirit, flow in the power of God, be anointed, be healed, be provided for, have a ministry, be successful. I really don't see what all the fuss is about with this intimacy stuff!" That is what the prodigal son thought. Initially, he only valued the Father for what He could do for him (give me, give me, give me), not for a relationship of love and intimacy.
>
> For many of us, love means pain. Those who have spoken the words to us, "I love you," seem to be the ones who have hurt and betrayed us the most. Others, who raised us and should have daily used healing words, never or rarely did. Then there were those who used words of love, but only when we performed correctly or lived up to their rigid standards. Some people said they loved us in order to get all of their needs met; they used us up and threw us away like dirty rags.
>
> No wonder so many people do not recognize or pursue their need for intimacy! We have hardened our hearts and conditioned our minds to believe that intimacy is something only a few weak people need. It is so easy to justify our lack of intimacy by thinking, "I wasn't raised that way. I had to be independent and self reliant. That's what

it takes to succeed. If anything is going to be done right, I'd better do it myself. You can't trust people. People will only hurt you. I'll not risk being hurt again. I'm no fool."

This type of thinking actually is rooted in fear, and fear is rooted in pride. It often hinders us from experiencing intimacy in the Father's love and with others. Pride is more concerned with what people think than with what God thinks. Pride is actually a fear of man. It is a fear of someone being able to hurt or have power over us. It cuts off the flow of intimacy. We start building walls of self protection and become a "news, sports, weatherman" (a superficial person who lets no one in). In Christian circles, pride often leads us to surrounding ourselves with religious language, duty, and activity. Intimacy then becomes something of which we feel we have no need. Then we never seem to find rest, security, or a place of comfort. We are left feeling like spiritual orphans and have to harden our hearts further and perform more so we can cover up the feelings of emptiness or pain.

True intimacy involves great faith, risk, and discomfort because of the word that I have found most people do not like: SUBMIT!!! Love and intimacy are something we have to submit to before we can receive them. We are willing to receive salvation. We are willing to receive the Holy Spirit. But few are willing to submit to love because love means pain to most folks. There seems to be a hidden trigger mechanism inside of us that activates each time someone gets too close, too real, too loving. This causes us either to shy away from intimacy and love or not to try to work hard enough to earn them.

Wives have been disappointed or wounded many times by their husbands when they draw too close to their husband's deepest feelings, only to have them harden their hearts or withdraw in anger.

To submit to love and intimacy is a humiliating thing. It always involves humility. Humility is a willingness to be known for who we really are and then be willing to change whatever is not Christ like. Humility is rooted in love and is the opposite of pride. It involves faith, which is the opposite of fear. We can risk walking in intimacy only when we have faith that is rooted and grounded in the Father's unconditional love for us.

What is Necessary for Me to Begin to Move Towards Deeper Intimacy?
First, you must become aware of your need for intimacy. Genesis 1:26 says that you were created in the image of God. 1 John 4:16 says that God is love. God's image is love! Do you see you yourself as being created by love, and for love, in order to spend your days receiving the Father's love so that you can give it away to your family and then His? "Love was not put into your heart to stay. Love is not love until it is given away!"

What is your image of yourself? The image we have of ourselves determines the depth of intimacy in which we dwell. Do you see yourself as a lover, one who is open, transparent, and shares intimately his emotions and feelings with family and friends? Do you see yourself as one in need of others in order to give away all of this love and intimacy you are experiencing in God? Or do you see yourself as independent, strong willed, in need of no one. "I'll not let someone else in or they will hurt me again." If you don't believe you are lovable, you find it difficult to receive God's gift of unmerited love and favor. And there is no way you can enjoy normal relationships with others if you view yourself differently from the way God views you.

Do you let people touch the deepest part of you, the tender and needy areas? Are you sensitive to others' needs and seek to meet them? Or are you more concerned with your own needs, successes, and ministry? Do you only allow family and people to touch the surface, while the real you remain hidden behind masks and pretenses? "Light reveals. Darkness hides. Whenever you do anything or say anything to hide what you are or what you have done, that is darkness." ("The Calvary Road" by Roy Hession)

Secondly, we must realize that our sense of value and self worth is based upon our ability to love. The way we think about ourselves is how we think God thinks about us. If we are uncomfortable with ourselves we are uncomfortable with others. Therefore, we must find our self worth in that for which God has created us intimacy and love!

We see in Genesis 2:18 that it was not good for Adam to have intimacy with God alone. So God gave Adam the ability to commune with nature and animals (vs. 19 & 20), yet Adam still was not secure and complete. God is helping Adam to become aware of his need for more than communion with God and nature. Man is becoming aware of his need for oneness with a woman. Until Adam saw this, he could not be trusted with a woman. Today, until men see their need for intimacy with God and family more than sports, nature, business, and ministry it is difficult for them to be trusted with a woman. They may use them, bruise them, and blame them for all the frustration and insecurity that comes when men do not find their value and self worth in intimacy with their wives, God, and others.

Paul made it clear in Ephesians 5:25-28 that men will not love and value themselves until they begin to love, cherish, cleanse, heal, and restore their wives through intimacy. Until a man moves towards intimacy in relationships, he will be insecure, and he will try to find his identity in the world or a religious system. If a man does not feel like he is the greatest husband on earth, his marriage is in trouble. He is not doing what God created him to do. To be a lover who is full of passion and intimacy. There are those who say that men live out of their mind and are task oriented while women are feelers and more relational. We've embraced the lie as truth and we are in bondage to it. It has held men back from intimacy. Jesus was the greatest lover, feeler, and compassionate man that ever was on earth. He was sensitive to His bride's every need. Men are to love their wives and others as Christ did. Christ lives in us and we have been empowered to walk in the love and intimacy and care that He did, if we so choose!

What if on the day of the great white throne judgment you are asked only one question? Jesus looks you in the eye and then speaks to your wife, "Did your husband love you as I loved the church and gave My life for it? " What would her answer be? It is one thing for her to hear the words, "I love you!" It is another thing for her to believe it. If she does not believe it, maybe it is because you have looked for value, security, identity, and passion outside of the home. Then she never has been able to receive your love. Therefore, she has been left uncovered, unprotected, and unhealed.

You can never stand before God and say, "I was never loved in my youth so I could not express love to others!" You cannot use this as an excuse because the Father has said to you, "I have loved you with an everlasting love; I have drawn you with loving kindness." (Jeremiah 31:3) You have been loved, but have you been willing to submit to it? His love is more powerful than all of your pain. All you have to do is to lower your walls, fears, and excuses and yield to love and intimacy. When you begin to do so, you will be surprised how easily love transforms you.

It is against the laws of nature and creation for you not to walk in love and intimacy. It is the most natural thing in life you can do when you submit to love. You are created in God's image of love. You are made for love and intimacy! It is your destiny! You have been created as a gift of love to this world! As you yield more deeply to the Father's love, it will flow through your spirit, and you will begin to supply your family and the world with love and intimacy! The world will never be the same again![52]

> Two are better than one because they have a good return for their labor. For if either of them falls, the one will lift up his companion. But woe to the one who falls when there is not another to lift him up. Furthermore, if two lie down together they keep warm, but how can one be warm alone? And if one can overpower him who is alone, two can resist him. A cord of three strands is not quickly torn apart *(Ecclesiastes 4:9-12).*[53]

According to Christian Healing Ministries School of Healing Prayer on Intimacy in Relationships:

> ...the emphasis is on relationships. Union with God and then union with one another. We must become aware of our need for intimacy. God called us to love one another and to bear one another's burdens, to care for one another, to go the extra mile, to be the Good Samaritan, to lie together, to walk together, and to eat together. In Janet Woititz book, "Struggle for Intimacy," she defined intimacy as "a love relationship with another person where you offer, and are offered, validation, understanding, and a sense of being valued intellectually, emotionally and physically." I have added "spiritually. We see all the time where it is not happening all around us, and perhaps in our own relationships where one person takes control, takes charge in the relationship. Their opinion is the only one that counts; they move into the driver's seat, into controlling.

We must be willing to embrace our responsibility for intimacy. When intimacy does not exist, it creates a vacuum at the heart of the relationship. This can be in a marriage. It can be in a friendship. It can be in a church. When there is a vacuum, invariably something comes in to fill that vacuum. So if you have this vacuum at the heart of your relationship, something is going to go in and fill it

We need to be able to talk to each other, and in order for there to be intimacy between the sexes; it needs to be without it always being sexualized. If it is impossible for me, in a relationship, to talk about my needs, to talk about my dreams, to talk about my desires, to talk about whatever it is that I am going through, then I am not in an intimate relationship.

We are all programmed to want to be perfect, and it is really difficult to break out of that. You will never have an intimate relationship with another person if you demand perfectionism of yourself or of the other person. Honesty is at the heart of every intimate relationship. It's at the heart of it. And without it, and without permission to be flawed, and to be broken, and to be afraid, you will never have an intimate relationship.

You have to have a minimal amount of trust in someone before you can move to intimacy with them. Intimacy is being able to be yourself with another person. Trust is formed early in life. It is given to us as a gift. If it is not given to us early in life, we do not trust anyone, and we are very suspicious. Some people move all the way into paranoia. The majority of us are afraid of relationships. We are afraid of people. What will he think? What will she think? How did they express intimacy with you?

Intimacy requires us to find our value and self worth in being who God created us to be. What is your self image, the true self or the false self? The false self cannot love. The false self always seeks to control, lives in illusions and preoccupations—never in the moment, never in the now. The false self is birthed in fear, has limited communication, and is not capable of intimate relationships. The false self is also shame based. Everything they perceive about themselves, they take from their outside environment. Better looking, better job, better car, etc.

When we start living from what is inside ourselves, we are living with the true self. A relationship with God, a relationship with ourselves, our strengths, our love relationships. The true self has an intense capacity for love and connectedness. It has no need to control, none whatsoever. It gives freedom. It lets that person come and go. It is rooted in truth, birthed in love, created by God, birthed by parents that loved and affirmed. It is capable of deep intimacy.[54]

As Dr Grant Mullen expresses in his book *Why Do I Feel So Down When My Faith Should Lift Me Up?*:

When the emotional adolescence remains unhealed, people hate themselves and become preoccupied with their own sense of emptiness, guilt, shame, and inadequacy. Unfortunately, most of us are still struggling with this phase and these unhealed immature emotions.

Childhood and adolescence are the times of greatest vulnerability to rejection since it is the time when people need repetitive reassurance to build confidence and a healthy self image. The more cold and rigid a family is, the more fear and rejection the members will experience. Childhood rejection leaves very deep and lasting wounds.[55]

Through the rest of high school, I experienced events that just solidified what a failure I was. The girl that was my on stage dance partner when I was seven years old became a student at my high school. From the very first day she would not talk to me or recognize me. She became one of the popular girls in school and totally rejected that I even existed. I never knew why until our 25th class reunion, when she said I was the first person to break her heart. She said that she had sent me letters after my mom died but that I never wrote back. I am sure that my aunt never gave them to me. I was not allowed to have a normal social life.

As a teenager, I was not allowed to have friends over and was never allowed to have sleepovers. We just didn't want anyone to know our business. I never learned how to be sociable like other teenagers my age. We had to keep all the window blinds closed so that the neighbors couldn't see in. When we traveled, we weren't allowed to stay at anyone's house because it was not proper to impose on people. That was not the right thing to do. This just reinforced that having intimate relationships was not the right way of life.

The few relationships I had with girls in high school thoroughly undermined my confidence in my ability to ever have a satisfying sexual relationship. My aunt made it abundantly clear to me that I was not ever to get a girl pregnant while living in her house. When the opportunity for heavy kissing presented itself in these relationships, an orgasm before the possibility of intercourse ended the evenings. I was in a major panic. With my scientific perfectionist mind, I researched every book I could find. In the 1960s, the bible of sexual behavior was the Kinsey report. From reading it, I determined that the purpose of the male was to sexually satisfy the female. That this was intimacy. Inability to accomplish this was dysfunctional and needed medical attention. I concluded that I was sexually dysfunctional. I lost any sexual confidence that I should have had or could have had. I was damaged goods. No women would ever love me now. This is the kind of thing you don't talk about to anyone. Unfortunately, back then we didn't have people like Dr. Oz or Dr. Berman to clearly explain things about sex. Apparently that need still exists today. So again, another situation that reinforced my feelings that I was not lovable and could never be loved. I now felt I was a failure as a man and that I could never experience an intimate relationship with a woman. This proved to be devastating to the success of all future relationships in my adult life. We knew nothing about storge love depravation during the 1960s. There was nothing in literature about it at that time. We will discuss it later in this book.

COUNTERFEIT PASSIONS

We as orphan hearts start looking for love in all the wrong places. These affections can be passions, possessions, position, performance, people, place, and power.

Passions

> We seek Passions because we are lonely and insecure. We seek to fill these needs through other means that often develop into...addictions to food, alcohol, drugs, sex, pornography, and whatever else comforts us.[56]

With no confidence in myself and feeling that I would fail in relationships with women, I turned to counterfeit passions. It didn't take me long to drown myself into the numbing affects of alcohol. Alcohol also gave me the courage to pursue relationships that would always end up in the same self crash and burn destruction. I did go to college for pre med because of the directive to study hard and become a doctor my mother had cursed me with. It turned out that I was good in math and science, but even better at partying 101. I did not make the grades necessary for med school, but instead graduated with a degree in Biology. Another failure in the list of failures in my life. When I finally did marry, all the elements were present to destroy the marriage. My orphan spirit was afraid to trust, afraid of rejection, afraid to receive love, afraid of intimacy, and could not unconditionally express love. My lack of sexual confidence spilled into the bedroom along with continued sexual dysfunctions. I could not communicate with my wife about this, so I would go to the bar every night after work and drink away the pain, hoping that when I got home my wife would be asleep. Besides, at the bar I was surrounded by bar room friends that liked me. We had the same interests. We could get drunk together, play pool together, laugh together, and have fun together. This lasted for eleven years until my wife could no longer live with constantly feeling rejected. She was living in a house where she felt unloved and very lonely. She did not have the intimate relationship that she needed and that I was not able to give to her. Unfortunately, in a divorce, society usually puts the blame on the female and believes that it is her fault for not keeping the marriage together. In reality, it was entirely my fault, not hers. It was because of an orphan spirit attitude that had become a stronghold in my life. I still had not found the Father's love. Remember, only the love of Father God can displace an orphan spirit. I had thrown him out of my life. I considered myself to be an agnostic.

Your spouse cannot ultimately meet your need for intimacy. If you are expecting him or her to give you all the love you need, when they are unable to do so, you will become vulnerable to defilement by someone else with an unmet love need. The kind of sacrificial love that a marriage requires can flow only out of the love that comes from the Father's embrace, from a relationship first established with God, from abundantly receiving His love, and then giving it away to your spouse. Until you value intimacy and love more than what God can do for you, you will continue to have a void in your heart. And, as in the laws of nature, wherever there is a void, something will try to fill it. Some people try to fill this void with alcohol, with drugs, or even with religion. But the longing and emptiness in your heart cannot be filled by anyone or anything except a relationship with the Father built upon love and intimacy, not duty and works. Until you have experienced this, it may be difficult to experience a truly intimate relationship with another person.[57]

Deeply intimate relationships with other people are possible only between individuals who are secure in God's love, because the foundation of such relationships is love, trust, and commitment. As soon as distance from God's unconditional love and insecurity begins to occur, intimacy with others becomes very difficult because we treat others in the way we feel about ourselves. Whatever we feel that we have to do to feel valued by God, then others will have to do the same to feel valued by us.[58]

This intimacy problem existed in every relationship I encountered for the next 20 years. After my divorce I again became the prodigal son looking to fill the void in my life for love in all the wrong places. The feeling of being sexually inadequate would only reinforce fear of intimacy, fear of rejection, fear to give and receive love, and fear of failure. Women in general can be kind and forgiving. However, there are those that would make comments like, "Is that the best you can do?" "Sweetie, why did you waste my time?" or "You really ought to find a clinic that can help you." The current generation of women need to be more educated and understanding in their relationships and be knowledgeable of the psychological and emotional damage that can be done. Every one of my relationships ended in doom and gloom, including the two that I really wanted to work. However, I was unable to give and receive love, I was unable to be intimate in the relationships, and I was now very much an alcoholic. Happy Hour after work was costing me $125-150 a week, and my credit card debt was astronomical.

Position and Performance
Position is achieved when we win the approval of others. We constantly seek affirmation that we are worthy, have value, and are accepted by others. We have a need to fit in.

Performance often leads to becoming a perfectionist. In order to feel good about ourselves, we constantly have one more thing that we must do. When we finally accomplish completion of an activity, it never is perfect enough, and so we raise our expectations to be more perfect. Therefore, reaching our final goal is never attainable.

We are all programmed to want to be perfect, and it is really difficult to break out of that. You will never have an intimate relationship with another person if you demand perfection of yourself or of the other person. In relationships I felt I had to be the perfect lover. The fear of not being a perfect lover was always there. I never could find happiness and love in relationships. In my work place I always had to be the employee that did a perfect job and wrote the perfect project report. If it wasn't perfect enough, I would do it over and over again to try to get it perfect. However, other employees who seemed to waste time, stood around to chit chat, accomplished less work, and made many mistakes were the ones who were getting the promotions and raises. I never could understand that. So I would work harder to become more perfect.

Place

We use our place in the workforce to fulfill our need to be happy. If only I had a better job. If only I lived somewhere else. If only I could run away. However, with each new job, each relocation, it doesn't take long before we are into the same rut. Our happiness erodes and again we start seeking to find ways to fill it.

I never could seem to attain happiness in the workforce. I worked twice as hard as everyone else never taking the time talking to people, because I had a job to get done. I was the perfectionist and I knew I was doing a better job than anyone else. I never could understand all those poor performance reviews throughout my career. Everyone else was getting the raises and I wasn't. If only I had a better job, or a different supervisor, or I lived somewhere else. Every time things would start to go badly with the job and company I was working for, I would start looking and send out resumes to other companies and other cities. With each new job I ended up being in the same situation after only a few months.

> People in our lives are there for only one purpose and that is to fulfill all our needs. This path leads us away from making God's Love our primary source.

From Jack Frost's *Would You Rather Be Right Or Have a Relationship*, Shiloh Place Ministries:

> ...in God's Word, He often turns what seems right and fair upside down. That is because it is Satan who demands what is right and fair. He demands payment for our sins and is constantly pronouncing us "guilty, guilty, guilty." But it is God who does not want to give us what we deserve. He wants to give us an undeserved, unmerited gift. Satan traffics in law and in what is right and

fair, what we deserve. God traffics in grace and mercy, what we do not deserve. Grace is a higher place than what is right and fair, and Satan can never operate in grace, only in accusations.

Satan is known as the "accuser of the brethren." His thoughts are always negative, accusatory, pointing out others' faults, blaming others, devaluing, and demanding of rights and justice. Resentment, bitterness, and a heavy heart follow Satan's thoughts.

"God is love" and He is the opposite of Satan. His thoughts are always positive, comforting, edifying, encouraging, accepting, valuing, and loving. Grace, forgiveness, and innocence follow after God's thoughts. "For I know the thoughts that I think toward you," saith the Lord, "thoughts of peace and not of evil." (Jeremiah 29:11).

We would receive hurt from people and our response would be for justice and what was right and fair. We acted more like God's policemen and would begin to develop accusatory thoughts or words about those who hurt us. Then we would become negative, critical, and devaluing towards them in our thought life. We did not realize it, but we were coming into agreement with Satan's thoughts with our own thoughts, and it brought us under judgment and hindered us from receiving healing and the blessings of God in our lives, families, and ministries. "But I tell you that anyone who is angry with his brother will be subject to judgment." (Matthew 5:22).

After all, when people mistreat and disappoint us, it is only natural to feel hurt and wounded. But do we respond with grace, "Father, forgive them, for they know not what they are doing! They are only acting out of their own hidden core pain and rejection! Help me to cover them and restore relationship!" Or do we demand vindication, trying to justify and clear ourselves from blame? Do we try to make ourselves look good and innocent by exposing and talking about others' faults and thus making them look bad or in error?

Vindication can be one of the hungriest, most destructive appetites we possess. VINDICATION IS ROOTED IN DEMANDING OUR RIGHTS AND JUSTICE FOR THE WRONGS DONE TO US! But God says, "Vengeance is Mine." It is His right and it will cost us dearly to try helping Him out. When we do, God backs away from the situation and lets us handle things in our own fleshly, accusatory ways. Unknowingly, we are actually coming into agreement with Satan and separating ourselves from intimacy with God and from our inheritance in His blessings. When we decide we had better do something to help God, God help us!

It is not a matter of what we want to give to someone who hurts us. It is a matter of what we want to receive. Do we want to receive a hardened wounded heart that separates us from an intimate relationship with God and leads us into resentments, pride, and anxieties? Or do we want to enter into God's rest and walk in the joy of a lifestyle of forgiveness that produces a meek and gentle spirit? When we choose our response to wounding situations, we also choose our future rewards. "Give, and it will be given to you; good measure, pressed down, shaken together, running over, they will pour into your lap. For by your standard of measure it will be measured to you in return." (Luke 6:38) The context of this verse is not about money but about how we respond to those who hurt and disappoint us.

We make the decision whether to receive mistreatment at the hands of others as a blessing or as a curse. God has promised a blessing if we respond with forgiveness and grace. But when we respond with accusation, vindication, fault finding, or blame shifting, we then give Satan a key to our front door and he can come and go as he pleases in our house (Ephesians 4:26-27).

"Blessed are you when men cast insults at you, and persecute you, and say all kinds of evil against you falsely, on account of Me. Rejoice, and be glad for your reward in heaven is great. But I say to you, love your enemies, and pray for those who persecute you in order that you may be sons of your Father who is in heaven; for He causes His sun to rise on the evil and the good, and sends rain on the righteous and the unrighteous. For if you love those who love you, what reward have you." (Matthew 5:11-12, 44-46).

These verses imply that there is no blessing or reward when we do good to good people. Blessing comes when we do good to the people who hurt us. The blessing is sonship! We end up with the feeling of full acceptance and unconditional love with the Father. We begin walking in a deeper intimacy with God and we start taking on His spirit of grace. That releases intimacy in most of our relationships. We then start becoming comfortable with love and forgiveness. This is the place where healing and the blessings of God begin to overtake you.

A study by Mark Virkler reveals that eighty percent of most Christian's thoughts are negative. "They didn't value me! They didn't speak to me! They were not concerned with my need! They! They! They!" You can take most of your thoughts or conversations about a difficult person in your life, and in one way or another line them up under one of two categories:

Thoughts of Restoration and Relationship or Thoughts of Vindication and Exposure
One way leads to blessing and the other way releases a self imposed curse. Satan wants us to inherit a curse. If the majority of our thoughts and conversations are in

agreement with him, he has a right to release the curse. "He also loved cursing, so it came to him; and he did not delight in blessing, so it was far from him. But he clothed himself with cursing as with his garment, and it entered into his body like water, and like oil into his bones." (Psalm 109:17-18).

God wants us to inherit a blessing. All we have to do is give the person a gift that they do not deserve, a gift of forgiveness and grace. "To sum up, let all be harmonious, sympathetic, brotherly, kindhearted, and humble in spirit; not returning evil for evil, or insult for insult, but giving a blessing instead; for you were called for the very purpose that you might inherit a blessing." (1 Peter 3:8-9).

It really comes down to this, WOULD WE RATHER BE RIGHT OR HAVE RELATIONSHIPS? How often our thoughts come into agreement with Satan when we strive to be right in our relationships, especially at home. The biggest problem is we usually are right about others' faults! But you can be right and have the wrong attitude and you are dead wrong. Jesus didn't "grasp" for position or authority (Philippians 2:5-8). Satan did. Jesus sought to humble Himself. Satan sought to exalt himself. Satan lost his position in God's presence. Christ was exalted to the right hand of the Father. When you choose the behavior, you choose the consequences!

Jesus revealed the path to blessing and intimacy in Luke 6:27, 28, 35: "But I say to you who hear, love your enemies, do good to those who hate you, bless those who curse you, pray for those who mistreat you and your reward will be great, and you will be sons of the Most High."

Love your enemies and you take on the spirit of Christ!

Do good to those who hate you and you may make them your friend!

Bless those who curse you and you inherit a blessing!

Pray for those who mistreat you and you see them through the loving eyes of the Father!"

Jesus walked out these principles with the one who hurt Him most, Judas. He knew what was in Judas' heart from the beginning, yet Jesus continued to serve and minister to him for three years. He allowed Judas to minister beside Him. He washed Judas' feet right before the betrayal. He broke bread with him and lived faithful to the covenant of loyalty with Judas in spite of Judas' actions towards Him. He never stopped receiving and valuing Judas.

Have you received the difficult person whom God has placed in your life as an instrument of blessing? If you do not value and respect them, then you may be treating them like a curse, thus inheriting a curse! When we receive them as a blessing to help us find out what is in us, then God can take every negative relationship and use it to bring us into spiritual maturity. This releases us to be an instrument of His love to our family and to the nations!

"And as for you, you (Joseph's brothers) meant evil against me, but God meant it for good in order to bring about this present result, to preserve many people alive." (Genesis 50:20)[59]

I used to brag to everyone I worked with that I was the type of the person who shot straight from the hip. I was proud that I would tell it like it is. If it looked like cow poop, smelled like it, felt like it, stuck to the wall like it, then it wasn't peanut butter no matter how much you wanted it to be.

Just recently in a conversation with one of my cousins I found myself again proving that a statement she made was totally wrong and not logical. If there is one thing that really irritates me, it is people that make statements that challenge logical thinking. For example, if someone said,

"Well, I saw a beagle peeing on a car tire and therefore I wouldn't want to own a beagle, because it would pee on car tires," this kind of logic would trigger an immediate response from in me to prove that that person is wrong and has a low IQ. So my cousin proceeded to tell me that her husband's cousin placed his career first on his list of priorities, owning a house second, and then getting married third. However, he never got married and so the person I knew that was doing the same thing will never get married. I immediately pointed out to her that just because her husband's cousin did that doesn't mean that every other guy is going to do the same thing; in short, that her statement was stupid. Was it more important to be right or to have a relationship? My cousin immediately moved across the room and started a conversation with another relative.

Power
Power seekers are the controlling people that seek to control their own lives and destiny. They seek to control emotions, people, or circumstances in order to never be disappointed or hurt again.

All you have to do is take a look at world leaders to get a good picture of this, especially the dictators of today and of the past. Just consider Hitler, Stalin, Castro, and Saddam Hussein, for example.

Perfectionism
We develop a "my way or the high way" attitude. If anything is going to get done and done right, I am going to have to do it myself.

As a perfectionist, I knew deep down inside that no one could do a better job than me and that everyone else was just a bunch of bungling idiots. If I let someone do a job, I usually took over to do it my way. I needed to be in control of the situation so that the outcome would produce the results I wanted.

Control and Oppression

We become controlling in our relationships. We limit our relationships and conversations to "safe" topics like the news, sports, weather, etc. The fear of trusting, fear of rejection, and fear of intimacy prevent us from tackling deeper subjects and from allowing anyone to become more personal with us.

The stronghold of oppression sets in. We constantly seek fulfillment in things that will never satisfy us. Because we cannot receive love, acceptance, and admonition from God or from others, our lives come under oppression of tension, anger, bitterness, restlessness, and frustration that has the potential to develop into depression.

We enter into a life as a spiritual orphan. An orphan heart feels that it does not have a safe and secure place in a father's heart where it is loved, valued, and affirmed.[60]

Chapter Three
The Orphan Spirit Attitude

An orphan spirit is not a spirit being or entity that can be cast out in the name of Jesus Christ, as cannot the spirit of justice, the spirit of the game, in the spirit of friendship, in the spirit of the children, in the spirit of the season, in the spirit of Christmas, etc. An orphan spirit attitude is the mood, attitude, intent, principle, and soul of the condition.

Jack Frost writes in *Spiritual Slavery to Spiritual Sonship*: "Many orphans during childhood development establish an orphan heart/orphan spirit. The orphan spirit is a heart attitude...(how the heart feels)...and a mental stronghold...(what the mind thinks from the input of these feelings...that is a temptation for all of us...[61] This describes the orphan spirit—independent; hostile; contentious; with no sense of home, belonging, or of being a son...[62]

The orphan spirit is not something you can cast out because the orphan spirit is ungodly beliefs and/or attitudes of our flesh that has been developing over a lifetime. It has become part of our personality and character. It must be displaced (put to death) by a personal experience in the Father's love and a revelation of the spirit of sonship. This will require a repositioning of our life. Peter Lord recently said, "If you keep doing what you have been doing, you're going to keep getting what you already got!"

So what are the hallmarks of an orphan spirit? Inability to have lasting relationships, hatred of authority, general distrust for leaders general lack of direction for your life, inability to make key, strategic decisions, drawing near, then backing away from intimacy, a sense that they're just going to reject you anyway, a gnawing sense of failure, never quite good enough, an inexplicable drive to succeed, win, prove yourself.[63]

To affirm you are lovable and capable of being loved. Your daddy wasn't around to tell you that.

All of these have developed out of an orphan heart attitude that has become a stronghold of oppression in an orphan's life.

According to Rev. David Kirschke of Lifeway Church:

> The orphan heart sees things differently than those with the heart of a son. An orphan spirit does not have a safe and secure haven in God. He or she must strive for self, and hold tightly to what he has. The spirit of a son, in contrast, has a spirit of submission to the will of the Father (John 5:19).
>
> "Home" is where you are loved unconditionally. If you don't have a "home", a safe and secure place, you have to live life looking out for yourself, for number one, because no one else will.
>
> There is a 12-step progression in developing "alienated affection":
>
> 1)   You focus on the faults of those in authority over you.

2) You become disappointed, discouraged, and wounded in spirit.
3) You lose trust in authority.
4) You fear submission to receive love, comfort, and admonition from parents.
5) You close your spirit to those in authority in your time of need.
6) You develop an independent spirit.
7) You begin to control relationships with anger, passivity, or isolation.
8) Your relationships become superficial.
9) You find that you have very few supportive relationships.
10) You begin to live life like an orphan, looking out for yourself.
11) You begin to find false comfort and identity in possessions, drugs, the praise of men, and so on.
12) You become a person who has great difficulty in receiving love and acceptance from either God or man.

When things go wrong, we try to handle things ourselves (orphan spirit) instead of throwing ourselves upon God (spirit of son).[64]

In "Dealing with an Orphan Spirit" Robert Holmes suggests:

...perhaps you had an absent father, or abusive mother. Perhaps you raised yourself because of the financial condition of your family, or the number of children in the home. On the spiritual side, neglect happens at every level in institutional Christianity. Leaders demand instead of admonish, berate instead of beseech, are busy with church life instead of the life inside the people, and are not being fathered by the system themselves. There are promises of parental love, but in reality, scarce little more than a request for the tithe.[65]

Leif Hetland of Global Mission Awareness teaches on his DVD, "Healing the Orphan Spirit":

When we are afraid of intimacy (in to me see), we put on FIG LEAVES such as Fear, Insecurity, Guilt, Loneliness, Escapism, Anxiety, and Failure. You are covering up. You no longer are able to see Father God's face clearly, hear His voice clearly, and feel His love. Christians may *fear* rejection, by God or by other Christians. They may *fear* failure, which can render them incapable of moving ahead in intimacy with God. This then leads to *insecurity*. *Guilt* and self condemnation are consequences of unconfessed sin that requires repentance. Without the Father's love, one feels a sense of *loneliness* and isolation, which can cause us to turn to *escapism*, seeking comfort wherever it can be found. When there is unresolved sin in a person's heart, *anxiety* will simmer just below the surface. All these consequences of sin cause a vicious cycle of further *failure*. You go after passions: You don't have His security, so you go after possessions. You don't have His values, so you go after position. The orphan spirit is about me, me, me. We set ourselves up to perform for what we want thereby establishing a performance habit. We come to perform for a promise and we end up with an Ishmael (orphan heart). We are not very good receivers, but instead we are very good achievers. However, there is a father hunger in our lives. Many of us see Father God as an authoritative Father and find it difficult to climb up onto His lap to receive His love. Especially if we think that He is mad and angry at us, if we think we need to perform to please Him, or if we are afraid of getting hurt. Father God wants us to be able to sit in His lap and experience being sons and daughters of a loving Father. He wants His family back and He wants to adopt us into His glorious family.

You are my beloved son and daughter in whom I am well please. This provides healing by:

1) Breaking the rejection you have experienced in your life.
2) It establishes roots of belonging. I am His.
3) You getting adopted in the beloved.

The spirit of Ishmael (the orphan heart) warring against the spirit of Isaac (the spirit of a son) seems to be the dominating spirit upon the earth today. The same spirit that is releasing terrorism upon the earth is also prevalent within all of society. Rivalry, envy, and jealousy produce violence within both the natural and spiritual realms as we compete with one another for the hearts of people and seek to establish our own land. Our search for acceptance, significance, and identity often results in a wrestling match as we grasp for what we deem is rightfully ours. It is evident within politics, the workplace, the entertainment and sports industries, and sadly, even within the Church. The result can be a "holy war" unconsciously proclaimed by those with an orphan heart as they struggle with their brethren for position, and authority, and inheritance.

Jack and Trisha Frost write in *From Slavery to Sonship, Part 2:*

Ishmael (meaning "whom God hears") was the first born of Abraham to Hagar, the handmaiden of Sarah, Abraham's wife. At 16 years of age, Ishmael was forced into the wilderness, away from his father, because of jealousy and rivalry between the two women over whose son would have rights to the inheritance of Abraham

(Genesis 21:9 21). Arabic historians divide the Arabs into two races: (1) Pure Arabs, descendants of Joktan; and (2) Mixed Arabs, descendants of Ishmael. The prophecies from Genesis 16:12 and 25:18 are now and have always been true: "And he (Ishmael) will be a wild donkey of a man, his hand will be against everyone, and everyone's hand will be against him. He settled in defiance of all his relatives." Since the moment Ishmael experienced rejection from his father through the next 3,900 years, many of Ishmael's descendants' attitudes, dispositions, manners, habits, government, or dress have not changed. What also has not changed is the tension between the one who lives life as if he does not have a home (the spirit of an orphan) and the one who is secure in his father's love and heart (the spirit of sonship).

Often within the church, it is difficult to tell whether a person walks in the heart attitude of an orphan or a son (this includes daughters). Outwardly, a person may have a pattern of service, sacrifice, discipline, and apparent loyalty, but you do not know what is inside a person until he or she gets bumped. Then the attitude of the heart overflows at a time when they feel they are not getting the recognition or favor they deserve. Somehow the difference lies in the motives and intentions of the heart. Let us look at the following chart and see what is revealed as we put definitions to the terms "spiritual orphan" and "spiritual son" and place them side by side in contrast with one another.

It is for discipline that you endure; God deals with you as with sons; for what son is there whom his father does not discipline? But if you are without discipline, of which all have become partakers, then you are illegitimate children and not sons. Furthermore, we had earthly fathers to discipline us, and we respected them; shall we not much rather be subject to the Father of spirits, and live? *(Hebrews 12:7-9)*

The Spirit of an Orphan		The Spirit of Sonship
See God as Master	**Image of God**	See God as loving Father
Independent / Self-Reliant	**Dependency**	Interdependent / Acknowledges Need
Live by the Love of Law	**Theology**	Live by the Law of Love
Insecure / Lack Peace	**Security**	Rest and Peace
Strive for the praise, approval, and acceptance of man	**Need for Approval**	Totally accepted in God's love and justified by grace
A need for personal achievement as you seek to impress God and others, or no motivation to serve at all	**Motive for Service**	Service that is motivated by a deep gratitude for being unconditionally loved and accepted by God
Duty and earning God's favor or no motivation at all	**Motive Behind Christion Disciplines**	Pleasure and delight
"Must" be holy to have God's favor, thus increasing a sense of shame and guilt	**Motive for Purity**	"Want to" be holy; do not want anything to hinder intimate relationship with God
Self-rejection from comparing yourself to others	**Self-Image**	Positive and affirmed because you know you have such value to God
Seek comfort in counterfeit affections: addictions, compulsions, escapism, busyness, hyper-religious activity	**Source of Comfort**	Seek times of quietness and solitude to rest in the Father's presence and love
Competition, rivalry, and jealousy toward tothers' success and position	**Peer Relationships**	Humility and unity as you value others and are able to rejoice in their blessings and success
Accusation and exposure in order to make yourself look good by making others look bad	**Handling Others' Faults**	Love covers as you seek to restore others in a spirit of love and gentleness

The Spirit of an Orphan		The Spirit of Sonship
See authority as a source of pain: distrustful toward them and lack a heart attitude of submission	**View of Authority**	Respectful, honoring: you see them as ministers of God for good in your like
Difficulty receiving admonition: you must be right so you easily get your feelings hurt and close your spirit to discipline	**View of Admonition**	See the receiving of admonition as a blessing and need in your life so that your faults and weaknesses are exposed and put to death
Guarded and conditional: based upon others' performance as you seek to get your own needs met	**Expression of Love**	Open, patient, and affectionate as you lay your life and agendas down in order to meet the needs of others
Conditional & Distant	**Sense of God's Presence**	Close & Intimate
Bondage	**Condition**	Liberty
Feel like a Servant / Slave	**Position**	Feel like a Son / Daughter
Spiritual ambition: the earnest desire for some spiritual achievment and distinction and the willingness to strive for it; a desire to be seen and counted among the mature	**Vision**	To daily experience the Father's unconditional love and acceptance and then be sent as a representative of His love to family and others
Fight for what you can get!	**Future**	Sonship releases your inheritance!

With the chart and scriptures listed, let's define the orphan spirit and the spirit of sonship. The orphan spirit causes one to live life as if he does not have a safe and secure place in the Father's heart. He feels he has no place of affirmation, protection, comfort, belonging, or affection. Self oriented, lonely, and inwardly isolated, he has no one from whom to draw Godly inheritance. Therefore, he has to strive, achieve, compete, and earn everything he gets in life. It easily leads to a life of anxiety, fears, and frustration.

The spirit of sonship is all about having a heart attitude of submission being subject to another's mission. Jesus Himself said, "The Son can do nothing of Himself, unless it is something He sees the Father doing; for whatever the Father does, these things the Son also does in like manner." (John 5:19). In Hebrews 12:9, "Be subject" is also the word for "submission." In the Greek, this word means "to get underneath and to push up." So to have the spirit of sonship is to put yourself underneath another's mission and do all you can to make them successful, knowing that as a son/daughter, there is an inheritance that lies ahead. Sonship is about security, significance, identity, patience, basic trust, faithfulness, loyalty, humility, and being others oriented

After reading through the contrast chart and definitions, you probably are saying to yourself, "Woe is me!" You may fit into only some of the categories, but most likely you will have some bleed over between the two. Now perhaps you can see why walking in healthy relationships with God and/or others has been so difficult for you or someone you know.[66]

We must first acknowledge our need for change. First, we could see no fault on our part because we worked so hard to do everything right...Second, we began to confess to one another the sins of the orphan spirit. As we began to acknowledge our impure motives, it was as if we stepped out of darkness and into the light...Third, we felt there was a need to receive forgiveness from those against whom we had sinned...Fourth, Trisha and I knew this would be a daily walk of repentance. The spirit of sonship was not a garment we put on, but it was a change of heart so deep that it brought change to our habits. A new passion was awakened within us to be a blessing in every way...Fifth, we received revelation on sowing into our inheritance. God soon branded on our hearts several verses: "For if the Gentiles have shared in their spiritual things, they are indebted to minister to them also in material things." "And let the one who is taught the word share all good things with him who teaches. Do not be deceived, God is not mocked; for whatever a man sows, this he will also reap. For the one who sows to his flesh shall from the flesh reap corruption, but the one who sows to the Spirit shall from the Spirit reap eternal life." (Romans 15:27; Galatians 6:6-8)...Sixth, we began receiving our inheritance. For so many years, we had fought and grasped for recognition and ministry. Then, as a passion for the spirit of sonship rose up within us, almost overnight the blessings of God came upon...us...[67]

A person with an orphan spirit attitude does not feel safe in the Father's love. This causes that person to strive and earn everything in life. A person with an orphan heart attitude is someone who does not feel they have a safe place in the heart of a loving earthly father. It is possible to have an orphan heart attitude and not an orphan spirit attitude and vice versa. It is also possible to have both. The orphan heart and orphan spirit must be displaced by a personal experience in the Father's love to achieve inner healing. The final result is the revelation of the spirit of sonship with Father God which is discussed in a later chapter.

Chapter Four
The Spiritual Orphan Attitude

Donna J. Kazenske writes in her article "Spiritual Orphans:"

What is a spiritual orphan? A spiritual orphan is one who feels alone; one who feels that they do not have a safe and secure place in the Father's heart where He can affirm, protect, provide, and express His love to them. They feel as if they do not belong. They are full of fear, anxiety, and insecurity.

Spiritual orphans cannot receive the love of the Father because they have been personally abused, hurt, rejected, and wounded by their earthly fathers or those in authority over them. They cannot receive the love of their heavenly Father because they cannot bring themselves to a place of being able to trust Him.

Trust involves vulnerability. Trust involves receiving. Spiritual orphans cannot trust or receive until the unhealed issues and hidden cores of pain are attended to. Basic trust is a real issue in the life of a spiritual orphan.

Trust involves opening your heart to others. Spiritual orphans have closed their hearts because they are afraid of being hurt. They refuse to make themselves vulnerable to others because of past hurts and pain. Their spirits are closed to a love relationship with their heavenly Father because they do not trust Him. Instead of running to God, they are continually running away from Him.

Spiritual orphans are dysfunctional because they lack the basic trust needed to have healthy relationships with those in authority. They find themselves battling with fear, control issues, independence, and pride. They are not able to have intimate relationships because they are not able to receive comfort or love from God or others.

Spiritual orphans are those who remain in the outer court of God's presence. They do not have the capability to enter into the Holy of Holies because they fear intimacy. They have closed their hearts as a type of protection.

They are not able to submit to authority because of fear. Submission involves having an open heart. Submission involves vulnerability, closeness, and honesty in relationships. Submission is an act of humility and receiving that releases God's grace and abilities in our lives. Submission has the power to set us free from our fears and insecurities.

Spiritual orphans have an independent spirit, which often causes them to hide or deny pain. They like to control relationships with anger, passivity, isolation or various other means. They keep their distance from those who are in authority or from those who are able to help them.

Spiritual orphans often find comfort and identity in money (by possessing material things), addictions (to alcohol, drugs, food and other forms of immorality), position (looking for acceptance by obtaining the praise of man or striving to be seen by man), and power (by controlling their own lives).[68]

Jack and Trisha Frost in their article "From Slavery to Sonship" write:

> To a Christian, home is where we can constantly hear the voice of our Father saying, "You are the child I love and in whom My favor rests!" When we feel we are truly at home in the Father's love, we do not constantly struggle with fears, anxieties, insecurities, lusts, addictions, compulsions, or aggressive striving. When we do not feel at home, secure and at rest in the Father's love, it becomes very easy to live our lives as if we do not have a home.
>
> We are left feeling like a spiritual orphan—feeling that we do not have a safe and secure place in the Father's heart where He protects us, affirms us, provides for us, expresses His love to us, a place where we belong.
>
> A spiritual orphan experiences the loss of "basic trust in parental authority." Basic trust does not mean the ability to believe or trust one another. It is the capacity to hold your heart open to others, especially if you believe another's motives or intentions are not pure. Basic trust is having an open heart. It is when you risk being vulnerable, even when it hurts you to stay open and not to close your spirit. Basic trust is when you are able to move beyond the weaknesses in others, receive God's healing touch one moment at a time, and not run away. You are able to risk being childlike again and receive love and nurture. Basic trust is foundational for building healthy relationships.
>
> Without basic trust, especially toward those in authority, relationships easily become dysfunctional: "I do not trust you enough to talk about my feelings." If you do not have basic trust, you may battle with pride, fears, independence, and control, thus finding great difficulty in receiving love and comfort from God and others. Intimacy is lost!
>
> A spiritual orphan has a fear of submission to receiving love, comfort, and admonition. Love, comfort, and healthy

admonition are all part of healthy relationships and are things to which we must be willing to submit. Submission is a Latin word that means, "to place yourself underneath and to push up at the same time." Submission is having an open heart which enables us to be close, vulnerable, and honest in our relationships."

Submission is an act of humility and receiving that releases God's grace and abilities in our lives and helps free us from our fears and insecurities with relationships (1 Peter 5:5-7). Fear of submission results in a closed spirit. This leads to an independent spirit: "I subconsciously cannot trust you to help me, so I would rather handle everything myself."

Independence often causes us to hide or deny our pain, so we begin controlling our relationships with anger, passivity, isolation, or "news/sports/weather" games. Our relationships become superficial as we fear truly opening our hearts to people because we fear being hurt again. Nobody really knows us. We especially keep our distance from those in authority or from the very ones who may be able to help us by providing comfort, wise counsel, love, acceptance, and/or belonging. We may find ourselves with very little healthy, supportive, and affirming relationships around us. We end up feeling alone and isolated, even around friends and family. We have fallen into the ungodly belief of living life like a spiritual orphan.

We are left feeling that we have no safe place, no one to care for our soul, no one we can trust to affirm and admonish us, no place to belong and be protected. So the spiritual orphan begins to find comfort and identity in one or more of the following counterfeit affections: possessions—finding security in money or things; passions—addictions or compulsions to alcohol, drugs, food, immoral issues, etc.; position—finding acceptance by striving to be seen or slaving for the praise of man; power—being in control of your own life and destiny.

The end result is a person who finds great difficulty receiving love, acceptance, and admonition from God and/ or from others, especially during times when they feel like they have failed or when they believe others have failed them. Because receiving is difficult for them, true intimacy is a fleeting thing, so they often focus their relationship with God upon His acts, gifts, discipline, duty, and/ or in hyper religious activity. They may not even be able to sustain a healthy relationship with God at all. Their relationships with others, especially within their family, often depend upon the others' performance. Because they may fear their own weaknesses being exposed, they may feel threatened or withdraw if others get too close to their hidden core pain. They tend to find it very easy to see others' faults and justify keeping a reserved distance by the weaknesses they see in others. They may be very subtle in criticizing or devaluing others, either in their thought life or in conversation.

Experiencing a revelation of the Father's love and living life as if we have a home is often hindered by our unhealthy fear of His discipline in our life (Hebrews 12:7 10).

When things seem to be going wrong, we subconsciously think it wise to keep our distance from others and from Father God and may try to handle the pain and disappointment ourselves. A lack of basic trust may be at the very root. As long as our image of Father God produces within us fear or condemnation and not compassionate, forgiving love, it becomes easy to act more like orphans (servants) than sons or daughters.[69]

Chapter Five
The Father's Blessing

Behold, I am going to send you Elijah the prophet before the coming of the great and terrible day of the LORD. He will restore the
hearts of the fathers to their children and the hearts of the children
to their fathers, so that I will not come and smite the land with a
curse *(Malachi 4:5-6)*.

We receive our father's blessing when our earthly
father affirms to us that we are lovable and capable of love. We go through our childhood with a Father
hunger wanting to hear the same words that the Father
said to Jesus in Luke 3:22, "You are my beloved Son (or
daughter); in you I am well pleased." Without the presence of our father, we did not learn how to receive love,
how to trust, and how to be intimate in relationships,
and therefore we became emotionally dysfunctional.
Our image of God is developed through our image of our
father. For war orphans, the image of a loving, caring,
and nurturing Father was fractured by the absence of

our earthly father. We then projected our image of our father onto God. Unfortunately, as adults, we pass on to our children what we learned as children, which then continues to be passed on from generation to generation. No one wins in war.

What are the results of not having an earthly father's love in a child's life?

John and Paula Sanford in their book *Restoring the Christian Family* **refers to a prison ministry for men by Mr. Carl Foss called "The Vision" which:**

> Reported that...90-95% of the prisoners never knew the love of a father...Studies...revealed that children raised without fathers commonly lack strength of character, lack "backbone," tend more to have sexually deviant behavior, and fall more easily into crime...In 1965 in America, 3,000,000 mothers were raising children without fathers, but by 1975, 10,000,000 were without fathers... The greatest tragedy of our materialistic culture is that men have been demeaned of their status as sons of God... they have little or no awareness of what they are to their children. Truly, Satan came to rob and to steal. Fathers' identities have been stolen from them!
>
> If a father fails to be with his child, that child's spirit withers...child must abide in his father's favor and love... Their love is not a nice addition; it is the *sine qua non*, essential necessity of a child's life. If fathers fail, substitutes can be provided... But no substitute can ever discover to a child the identity that calls from his *genes* to be realized... Girls who are raised with violent drunken fathers almost invariably marry violent, drunken men. Dominant, brutal fathers breed dominant, brutal sons and daughters whose husbands become dominant and brutal—unless the cross of Christ intervenes.[70]

An article by Leigh Dyer in the July 6, 2010 in edition of the *Charlotte Observer* **points out:**

> Recent statistics show that 40 percent of babies are now born to single moms; there's no reliable number for how many of those are single by choice rather than chance. But it appears certain that "choice moms" are a fast-growing category.

Jack Frost in "Experiencing Father's Embrace" writes:

> All human beings have four basic emotional needs. As children, we look to our parents and from three years of age especially to our fathers, to meet these needs for us. When these four needs are unmet in childhood, it becomes very difficult for a person to develop healthy relationships with God or with other people later in adulthood. They are:

1) The need for unconditional expressed love. It is not enough for a father to provide shelter, food, and clothing for his children. It is not enough for a father to have loving feelings for them. Those feelings must be communicated and expressed in a way that is meaningful to the child.

2) The need to feel secure and comforted. Every child needs to feel safe, both physically and emotionally. Children need to know that their families and households are emotionally safe, and that they always have a safe place in their father's heart, no matter how much they fail.

3) The need for praise and affirmation. Children will become better prepared for life when their self esteem and value are recognized and encouraged by their fathers.

4) The need for a purpose in life. Fathers have a respon-
    sibility to cultivate their children's talents and gifts.
    Everyone needs to find a sense of value, a belief that
    their lives mean something and that they can make
    a difference. Children need to be told that they are
    special, that they have something unique to offer the
    world, and that they are a gift of God's love to their
    family and to the world.[71]

In "Belonging" Sheila Linn examines what is affirmation?

Affirmation is not something that we do, but something that we are. It is a way of being present. The root of
the word affirmation is "firm." To...St. Paul affirmation
means to help the "hidden self" of another "grow strong"
or firm, through the quality of our presence (Eph. 3:16)....
Robert Bly has said...a boy receives food when he stands
in the shadow of his father. This is also true of girls and
mothers... People in the world...are starving for emotional
food... The most common hurt...seen in every country
where the...have given retreats is the lack of affirmation
in childhood... Many people have never had their goodness revealed to them by another person who loves them
unconditionally. We cannot affirm ourselves... We can
open ourselves to receive affirmation and we can build
upon what we receive, but first it is a gift that we receive
from others.

We cannot become our true selves until another person
affirms us. We become what others see in us. We become
our true selves when we see our goodness reflected back
to us in the eyes of another person who loves us...that we
have been born only once and we are still waiting for our
second, psychic birth, one that sufficiently affirms us, our
birth as our true selves.[72]

Dr. Conrad Baars has described how this happens in "Born Only Once":

I affirm another when I recognize that he is good, worthwhile and lovable precisely the way he is, period, without the usual addition of "in spite of his shortcomings," since that implies that my recognition and feeling of his goodness is conditional and that he must do something. And it is in and through the process of my being aware of, and my feeling of his goodness that I disclose the other to himself: "You are good the way you are; this is the way you may be; there is nobody like you; you are unique!"

I do not add, as is so often done, "I want to help you to become better," since that focuses on his not yet being better and creates in him a sense of being expected to do something in order to be better. The feeling that one is expected to do something stifles the opportunity for growing at one's own pace and in one's own way...

It is a process of affirmation, this process of knowing and feeling without doing, that I give the other to himself. I do not give him his physical existence as a human being. I give him his psychic existence as this specific unique human being."[73]

The critical time for psychic birth is around age two, when the child first experiences itself as a separate person.[74]

Sheila Linn writes in "Belonging" that she struggled most of her life with fear:

I was nearly always afraid, often to the point of terror... The situation in which I feel most frightened is when others speak critically or harshly to me. In the past, I tended to introject what they said, as if it were necessarily true, and begin speaking to myself even more harshly, using their words to beat on myself. Sometimes I would even begin to act like their negative view of me, although I knew it was not the way my real self would act. Then, I would get angry at myself for doing this. That only left me feeling worse about myself...I would then find ways to escape my pain, such as chronic busyness...[75]

In childhood, I...experienced...extreme verbal abuse. My mother screamed harsh words at me most of the time.[76]

During those years of fear I also felt lonely, insecure, inferior, and depressed. I felt that I did not belong. As if I belonged nowhere and to no one.[77]

For the first part of my life, I desperately needed to receive affirmation from other people who could give it.[78]

For many years I felt ashamed, frightened, lonely, insecure...as if I belonged nowhere and to no one. I tried healing through counseling...Unfortunately, psychotherapists are...trained in a method of traditional psychoanalysis in which the therapist remains emotionally distant from the client, an exaggerated form of "clinical distance"...However, the one thing needed by an orphan heart is...to be treated in a tender, motherly, (or fatherly) fashion, to be taken to another's heart...To be held in someone's arms and to feel that he/she belonged to someone and is loved and lovable. Ultimately it is love that heals.[79]

From Donna Kazenske's article on Spiritual Orphans:

Have you ever seen a hamster running around and around in a circular exercise toy? This type of activity is very similar to the lifestyle of a spiritual orphan. They have no sense of direction or destiny. They live their lives by just going through the motions.

Spiritual orphans are servants only and not sons or daughters of God. Servants perform duties, while sons and daughters receive the love of the Father.

I believe that we are in a season of becoming the true sons and daughters of God. The Holy Spirit is putting His finger in the hidden places of our hearts so that we can be healed and restored to a deeper relationship with Him. He desires more than an outer court relationship with us. He desires intimacy which involves inner court relationship. Inner court relationship involves trust and vulnerability.

Sonship is a matter of attainment and with it comes the privilege of authority in God. The body of Christ has not been fully operating in the authority of God because we are still functioning as spiritual orphans.

Jesus was declared the Son of God by His Father on the day of His baptism. Baptism represents death and resurrection. Baptism is a going down, a submitting unto death and an immersion into it. Resurrection can only take place after a death experience.

We must die to this orphan spirit. We must die to any independence of doing our own thing or doing our own will. We must die to any and all ungodly beliefs that keep us from becoming sons and daughters of God.

Spiritual inheritance is obtained only after death.

> When He had by Himself purged our sins, sat down at the right hand of the Majesty on high, having become so much better than the angels, as He has by inheritance obtained a more excellent name than they. *(Hebrews 1:3)*

What is this verse saying? What name did Jesus obtain through His death and resurrection? He obtained the name, "Son of God."

And the Holy Spirit descended in bodily form like a dove
upon Him, and a voice came from heaven which said, "You
are My beloved Son; in You I am well pleased." (Luke 3:22)

After Jesus was baptized, symbolizing His death and
resurrection, the Father made a decree from heaven to
the world that Jesus was His beloved Son.

The Father in heaven is now waiting to decree our
sonship not only to the world, but also to the principali-
ties and powers of hell. When God the Father decrees our
sonship as a result of our spiritual death and resurrection,
the demons in hell will tremble because we will walk in
the true authority and power of God.

It's time for us to get right with God. We need to repent
and receive forgiveness through His blood because we have
chosen to remain as spiritual orphans instead of sons and
daughters of God. We must allow the Holy Spirit to have
full rule and reign in our lives so that we can be set free and
healed by His supernatural power. We must give ourselves
completely to the Lord, withholding nothing from Him.

Therefore submit to God. Resist the devil and he will flee
from you. Draw near to God and He will draw near to you.
Cleanse your hands, you sinners; and purify your hearts,
you double minded. Lament and mourn and weep! Let
your laughter be turned to mourning and your joy to gloom.
Humble yourselves in the sight of the Lord, and He will lift
you up.[80] *(James 4:7-9)*

It wasn't until I had a life changing experienced of the
love of the Father that I set out on my own healing journey.
I was radically changed in 1989 at a conference in Miami,
Florida. I was at rock bottom, an alcoholic, out of a job, out
of money, losing my apartment, and had nowhere to go. I

was scouting bridges in the area with thoughts of becoming one of the homeless that sleep under those bridges. I even had several in mind. However, at a Holy Spirit conference, I was led by some unknown force to stand in line for prayer. When it became my turn, I said, "I have no idea why I am up here." While the prayer team prayed for me, I said, "God if you truly exist, give me a sign." Suddenly I felt as if a thousand volts of electricity shot through my body from head to toe. I stood there like a bawling epileptic that was having a seizure, totally out of control. From that day on, I was radically changed to become a born again Catholic. However, I continued to live with an orphan heart.

In 1995 the Lord woke me up in the middle of the night and in an audible voice told me he was calling me into healing ministry. I became a doubting Thomas and said, "I want confirmation from three people who don't know me to tell me to let my hands be Your hands." It wasn't long before I received those three confirmations in those exact words.

I became friends with Ellen who was on prayer team with me each month. At the time, I was praying to the Lord, "Please send to me the woman that you have chosen for me to spend the rest of my life with." Then Ellen would show up. I would again get on my knees and pray, "Lord can we talk, we seem to have a communication problem. Ellen is not the woman. You know my type, Christy Brinkley, Cheryl Tiegs, etc. Please show me whom you have chosen and make it abundantly clear." Ellen would show up. To take care of me when I had the flu, cook for me; invite me to her house, etc.

Unknown to me, she was praying to the Lord, "If this is the guy you want me to marry, have three people who know absolute nothing about what I am praying for give me each a red rose before the end of May."

We still have those three roses in a vase on top of the china cabinet. Yep, we got married, but I still had issues with an orphan heart and intimacy. Those issues were rooted in hidden core pain that I was not aware of.

Chapter Six
Our Image of God and How We See God

The healing of our orphan heart and orphan spirit is in direct relationship to our image of God. Many people still consider God as the punisher and enforcer Old Testament God. It is important to understand that the New Testament God is the all loving God. In history, healing the orphan heart and orphan spirit under Old Testament God mentality was hindered by a lack of understanding of the loving nature of God through his attributes. A full understanding of God's nature will expedite the inner healing process.

Pastor Harold Martin explains it this way:

> The orphan has a lifetime history of not being able to trust. Without understand the Fathering heart of God— how He desires to restore us to sonship—how and why He paid the price for our redemption and restoration— we will not be able to trust Him—without trust you will not receive.

In reality, there is no difference in the Old Testament vs. New Testament God . The difference is in our perception and our position. From the very beginning God has desired to be Father. We were created to be sons—the entire concept of sonship is His idea. Abba and Yahweh are the one and the same.

During Old Testament history healing the orphan heart was not achievable because what it took for Grace to become a reality in our life had not happened. The finished work of Jesus on the cross is what empowers the grace of God. Because the price of our sin—the cost of redemption has now been paid by Jesus—the Father can see—treat—respond and react to us as being righteous. The position of being righteous is the place of sonship. Old Testament people had servant—master mindset because that is what they were. Even the patriarchs considered themselves servants of God rather than sons. A son can serve but a servant can never be a son. True—many may have viewed God as vengeful and punishing but reality is what it took for adoption to become a reality was not available to them. A good servant would have viewed God as a good master—a poor servant would have viewed Him as a harsh master.

In "Agape Road" Bob Mumford examines the seven communicable attributes of God that are restored to us in Christ:

How God wants to be known

God's character or DNA is the content of His glory and the significance of His name. The breadth and meaning in these seven words that God uses to reveal Himself is spectacular. God's glory is the manifestation of His communicable attributes that are hidden from the world (see John 17:25). God is spirit; He cannot be known unless He chooses to reveal Himself."[81]

These are the aspects of Himself that Father God wants us to know about. God's seven communicable attributes are:

Compassion

Compassion: It is pity or empathy, inward affection, and tender mercy. The Greek word *splagchnon-splagkn'-non* is used 111 times in Scripture and means bowels of compassion or "mercy." Webster's dictionary defines compassion as...suffering with another; painful sympathy; a sensation of sorrow excited by the distress or misfortunes of another; pity; commiseration. Compassion is a mixed passion, compounded of love and sorrow; at least some portion of love generally attends the pain or regret, or is excited by it. Extreme distress of an enemy even changes enmity into at least temporary affection. Compassion means that my insides are moved for you in a supernatural way.

Grace

Grace: This is one of the most beautiful words in Hebrew, but it is not easily translated into English. This word is the very source of understanding God's person. It means to find favor, kindly, friendly, benevolent, courteous, disposed to show or dispense grace and forgive offenses, and to impart unmerited blessings.[82]

Grace is God doing for us what we cannot do for ourselves.

Patience

Slow to anger. Longsuffering is fortitude, forbearance, or patience. It means not being easily provoked and able to patiently bear injuries...It was anger that caused Moses, the meekest man on earth, to miss God's highest for his own life. When Moses struck the rock in anger (see Num.

20), it was a distortion of the glory of God. Moses misrepresented God as one who is easily angered. Amazingly, the water flowed irrespective of Moses anger; however, he was refused the privilege of entering the Promised Land with the people whom he had led. It is important to note that Moses did not lose his salvation—he appears later on the Mount of Transfiguration with Jesus, but he lost the opportunities and privileges that were part of his *earthly inheritance*. (added emphasis)

Mercy

Mercy: Mercy is mildness and tenderness of heart which disposes a person to overlook injuries or to treat an offender better than he deserves..."Be merciful, just as your Father is merciful" (Luke 6:36). The appeal is for us to reveal mercy because God is merciful. This is the essence of the Christian life, leading us on the journey to the freedom that He promised. The injury of the Church toward a hurting world has been failing to give mercy after receiving His mercy in such abundance. Behaving like this is a fast way to get into trouble with the Father.

Truth

Truth: Truth is conformity with fact or reality; exact accordance with that which is, has been, or shall be. Jesus said to him, "I am the way, the truth, and the life; no one comes to the Father, but through Me" (John 14:6). Truth is a person, the Lord Jesus Christ, who is the Word of God. "My mouth will utter truth" (Prov. 8:7a).

Faithfulness

Faithfulness: The Greek word is *hesed* meaning fixed, determined love, to be kept, guarded, watched over, and preserved. This is covenantal faithfulness. Once God gives Himself covenantally, it is impossible for Him to desert or abandon the person or the covenant. It is firm adherence to truth and duty, true to allegiance, careful to observe all compacts, treaties, or vows. In other words, true to one's word. God's affection is what makes the covenant.

Forgiveness

Forgive: This word means pardoning, remitting, disposed to forgive, inclined to overlook offense, mild, merciful, and compassionate as a forgiving temperament.

> Be gracious to me, O God, according to Your loving kindness; according to the greatness of Your compassion blot out my transgressions. Wash me thoroughly from my iniquity, and cleanse me from my sin. For I know my transgressions and my sin is ever before me *(Psalm 51:1-3).*

Sin has degrees of intensity and varying amounts of accountability which elicit different responses from Father God. Note the words: *iniquity, transgression, and sin,* and how David deals with each separately in Psalm 51. His iniquity is washed, his transgression is blotted out, and his sin is cleansed.

The first level is *iniquity.* There are 11 different words translated as "iniquity" in the Old Testament. The New Testament uses "lawless." The most prominent in the Old Testament is *awon* used 215 times, meaning crooked, that which is not straight, to bend, go astray, or deviation from the right path.

The second level is *transgression.* The word *transgression* occurs 80 times and its meaning is essentially a rebellious *attitude.* This is intentionally going beyond known limits, breaking or violating a law, principle, or relationship. It is deciding that the "No Parking" sign is for other people, not for us, so we intentionally go beyond the known limit and park there anyway.

The third level is *sin*. The Hebrew root of this word means "to miss the mark" or what is more commonly understood as failing, omitting, or refusing to do what we ought to do...Sin is used 430 times in both the Old and New Testaments and includes both Jews and Gentiles. To use the word *sin* is important because, unlike ignorance or chance, it involves some degree of choice, intention, and culpability...God forgives because it is His nature...The only part of the Lord's Prayer that Jesus took time and effort to more thoroughly explain was the urgent need for us to understand the necessity of forgiveness. "For if you forgive others for their transgressions, your heavenly Father will also forgive you. But if you do not forgive others, then your Father will not forgive your transgressions" (Matt. 6:14-15). When we receive forgiveness from the Father but refuse, withhold, or fail to give it to others, we may find ourselves in trouble with the Father. Many of us have serious difficulty forgiving. People do us wrong and we simply do not want to forgive them, yet we wrong others and then expect them to forgive us. We seriously jeopardize our journey toward intimacy when we refuse to forgive. Our stubbornness causes us to fail to reveal Father's hidden attributes to others and to misrepresent Him to those who are seeking to know Him. This we do much in the same way as Moses striking the rock in anger, misrepresenting the Father whom we serve.[83]

It is important that we have a current understanding of God and eliminate our Old Testament God mentality. Through studying the differences, we will achieve a healthy image of God.

Why is God so different in the Old Testament than He is in the New Testament?

In an article from Got Questions Ministries:

Why is God so different in the Old Testament than He is in the New Testament?, the article points out that at the very heart of this question lies a fundamental misunderstanding of what both the Old and New Testaments reveal about the nature of God. Another way of expressing this same basic thought is when people say, "The God of the Old Testament is a God of wrath while the God of the New Testament is a God of love." The fact that the Bible is God's progressive revelation of Himself to us through historical events and through His relationship with people throughout history might contribute to people's misconceptions about what God is like in the Old Testament as compared to the New Testament. However, when one reads both the Old and the New Testaments it becomes evident that God is not different from one Testament to another and that God's wrath and His love are revealed in both Testaments.

For example, throughout the Old Testament, God is declared to be "merciful and gracious, slow to anger and abundant in loving kindness and truth" (Exodus 34:6; Numbers 14:18; Deuteronomy 4:31; Nehemiah 9:17; Psalm 86:5; Psalm 86:15; Psalm 108:4; Psalm 145:8; Joel 2:13). Yet in the New Testament, God's loving kindness and mercy are manifested even more fully through the fact that "God so loved the world that he gave his one and only Son, that whoever believes in him shall not perish but have eternal life" (John 3:16). Throughout the Old Testament, we also see God dealing with Israel much the same way a loving father deals with a child. When they willfully sinned against Him and began to worship idols, God would chastise them, yet each and every time He would deliver them once they had repented of their idolatry. This is much the same way that we see God dealing with Christians in the New Testament. For example, Hebrews 12:6 tells us that "the Lord disciplines those he loves, and he punishes everyone he accepts as a son."

In a similar way, throughout the Old Testament we see God's judgment and wrath poured out on unrepentant sinners. Likewise, in the New Testament, we see that the wrath of God is still "being revealed from heaven against all the Godlessness and wickedness of men who suppress the truth by their wickedness" (Romans 1:18). Even with just a quick reading of the New Testament, it is evident that Jesus talks more about hell than He does about heaven. So, clearly, God is no different in the Old Testament than He is in the New Testament. God by His very nature is immutable (unchanging). While we might see one aspect of His nature revealed in certain passages of Scripture more than other aspects, He Himself does not change.

When one really begins to read and study the Bible, it becomes clear that God is the same in the Old Testament and the New Testament. Even though the Bible is really sixty six individual books, written on two (or possibly three) continents, in three different languages, over a period of approximately 1500 years by more than 40 authors (who came from many walks of life), it remains one unified book from beginning to end without contradiction. In it we see how a loving, merciful, and just God deals with sinful men in all kinds of situations. Truly, the Bible is God's love letter to mankind. God's love for His creation, especially for mankind, is evident all through Scripture. Throughout the Bible we see God lovingly and mercifully calling people into a special relationship with Himself, not because they deserve it but because He is a gracious and merciful God, slow to anger and abundant in loving kindness and truth. Yet we also see a holy and righteous God who is the Judge of all those who disobey His word and refuse to worship Him, instead turning to worship Gods of their own creation, worshiping idols and other Gods instead of worshiping the one and only true God (Romans 1). Because of God's righteous and holy character, all sin—past, present, and future—must be judged. Yet God in His infinite love has provided a payment for sin and a way of reconciliation so that sinful man can escape His wrath. We see this wonderful truth in verses like 1 John 4:10: "In this is love, not that we have loved God but that he loved us and sent his Son to be the propitiation for our sins." In the Old Testament, God provided a sacrificial system whereby atonement could be made for sin, but this sacrificial system was only temporary and merely looked forward to the coming of Jesus Christ who would die on the cross to make a real substitutionary atonement for sin. The Savior that was promised in the Old Testament is more fully revealed in the New Testament, and the ultimate expression of God's love, the sending of His son Jesus Christ, is revealed in all its glory. Both the Old and the New Testaments were given "to make us wise unto salvation" (2 Timothy 3:15). When we study them more closely, it really is evident that God is no different in the New Testament than He was in the Old Testament.[84]

OLD TESTAMENT GOD VS. NEW TESTAMENT GOD

From a quote posted on the blog Catholic Answers Forum:

The Old Testament is not Christianity, it is Judaism. The only reason the two are combined, is so that the first book, can explain the meaning behind the 2nd book, because they were written in the same context and within the same tribal community. The NT uses a lot of symbolism from the OT, because the writers of the NT were trying to appeal to the audience of the OT. They were trying to say this is the new way, for all humanity, not just the Jews. They were, however, talking to the Jews primarily when they wrote it. It wasn't made for the ears of a Gentile, because the Gentile did not understand its context.

There is a belief, that God "changed" his relationship with man, through Christ. Hence it is the same God with dramatically different behavior.

There is another view. Jesus disagreed with the Jews and their religion. They were wrong. Their view of God was not correct at the point in time Jesus was born, and Jesus taught about God, not about the Jewish God.

Throw that teacher into a very strict Jewish culture, and the writers of the Gospels had to appeal to the ancient texts and the culture of the day, or their message would never have been heard.

The two books are combined, because you cannot understand the 2nd, without the first, not because Jesus agreed with the 1st, but because the people who met him, had to communicate with those of the 1st.

That is the view I suspect is most accurate. Go and listen to a Jewish scholar on the NT, and you will see a whole different book (Dameedna).[85]

Why don't we see God acting the same now as in the Old Testament?

From a post to *The Virginian-Pilot* website Hampton-Roads.com:

Some believers...feel that main part of this answer is one of the more powerful truths in Christianity. That the reason we don't see the "God of Wrath" in the New

Testament and today is not because God has somehow changed, but because all the wrath that we deserve was poured out upon Jesus when he died on the Cross. He not only died for our sin, but also for the punishment of our sin. The reason that God poured out his wrath upon the Israelites is that when He looked at them, He saw their sin. But when God looks at us now, He doesn't see sin He sees His Son's blood wash away our sin. Paul, the author of 2nd Corinthians, wrote it this way:

Therefore, if anyone is in Christ, he is a new creation; the old has gone, the new has come! All this is from God, who reconciled us to himself through Christ and gave us the ministry of reconciliation: that God was reconciling the world to himself in Christ, not counting men's sins against them. And he has committed to us the message of reconciliation. We are therefore Christ's ambassadors, as though God were making his appeal through us. We implore you on Christ's behalf: Be reconciled to God. God made him who had no sin to be sin for us, so that in him we might become the righteousness of God. (2 Corinthians 5:17-21)[86]

Billy Graham posted his answer to "Is God in Old Testament Different from God in New?" on The Christian Post website. The Christian Post is an independent, pandenominational Christian media company that serves to provide direct and current news information to the general Christian public.

Q: Is the God you read about in the Old Testament different from the God of the New Testament? A friend of mine says that the Old Testament God is angry and cruel, while in the New Testament He is loving and kind. Is this true? D.McK.

A: No, it is not true. God never changes: He is the same today as He was 3,000 years ago, and He will be the same

3,000 years from now as He is today. As the Bible says, "I the Lord do not change" (Malachi 3:6).

The world does change, however, and it's true that God's people in Old Testament times faced different challenges from those their descendants would face. Often they were surrounded by hostile nations that were determined to stamp them out, and God said they must defend themselves against their enemies in order to survive. But repeatedly God assured them of His love; the prophet Jeremiah wrote, "The Lord appeared to us in the past, saying: 'I have loved you with an everlasting love; I have drawn you with loving kindness.'" (Jeremiah 31:3)

We see God's love most clearly, however, in the person of Jesus Christ. He was God in human flesh, who came down from heaven to express God's unchanging love to us. He did this by taking upon Himself the judgment we deserve for our sins, dying on the cross for us. The Bible says, "This is love: not that we loved God, but that he loved us and sent his Son as an atoning sacrifice for our sins" (1 John 4:10).[87]

Our false images of God come also from our parents. If God is a Father and our father was an alcoholic, what chance does God have to be a real Father? All parental love is human love. We get loved more if we are quiet, clean up, eat all our food, and help around the house. Because we expect to be loved not for who we are but for what we do, we begin to feel that we must also "merit" God's love. It's too much to believe that God's love is so different, an unmerited, unconditional gift giving power to love. Our image of God should mature as we grow but too often remains the same one we had when we were seven years old. Who was God then? The policeman, an unconcerned old man with a beard, a school teacher wanting perfection, the spoilsport sending suffering so that we could earn heaven, or the apathetic God who lets us down when we really need him? If God is not seen as the Being of light, then our view of life will not be a healing experience deepening our power to love and face death daily. We will remain crippled if we allow culture, parents, and childhood concepts to distort our image of God, making it impossible to give and receive enough trust and love. Our loveless culture and experience make contemporary man believe that God is not love.

Besides the wrong image of God, the second block to experiencing God's love is the wrong image of ourselves. God made man to his image and likeness. The real problem is not that we dislike God or our neighbor, but that we don't love ourselves. Due to the conditional love offered by parents and friends, we cannot love our limitations and weaknesses. We pay the price for not loving ourselves as much as God does. When we don't love ourselves, we behave in a way that makes it harder to love ourselves. We cover our insecurity by broadcasting our success, criticizing whoever isn't present, renting a dark corner for our shyness, becoming overextended and unable to say "no," criticizing ourselves to get sympathy, taking no risks that might fail, and agreeing with those who like the weather and those that don't. It is a vicious circle in which we become less lovable the less we love ourselves.[88]

Some of you may feel that you are a looser. Some of you may feel your life is hopeless. Some of you live in that lie without finding out the truth.

Story by Leif Hetland, Global Mission Awareness

> There is now biological proof that you are unique, a one of a kind winner. It has been reported that there are 50 million sperms cells on a race to reach the egg.

On their way they are bumping around, pushing each other aside. Finally one made it. And you won. You are the winner. You won the race. You are His. You are the son or daughter in which He is well pleased. Right now say this to yourself: I am His, I am His beloved, I am His beloved son or daughter, He loves me, He loves me and He is well pleased with me.[89]

From the book *Why Do I Feel So Down When My Faith Should Lift Me Up?* **by Dr. Grant Mullen:**

Our view of God's love will always be distorted by our view of our parent's love. As a result of the fall, sin entered the heart of man and the mirror cracked. Sin wounded mankind and contaminated our natures. We can never fully imagine the full extent of God's love for us since we have an imperfect human frame of reference as we look into a cracked mirror. Wounding experiences in our childhood damage our understanding and reduce our expectations of love. If for example, we have had a broken or damaging relationship with a father, not only will we have difficulty trusting human authority figures, but we will assume that God is as untrustworthy and damaging as our parent. This becomes a deep inner belief based on the lie that the father of lies plants at the time of the wounding. We then will have great difficulty trusting or becoming close to God *or anyone else*. When through this process we are unable to come emotionally close to God, then our relationship to him becomes solely intellectual.[90]

We need to heal our image of God within ourselves, within in our families, within our teenagers, within our societies, within our churches, within our cultures, and within our countries. We need to educate the orphans of the world that Father God loves them and that they are his sons and daughters in whom he is well pleased.[91]

From Shiloh Place Ministries. Experiencing Father's Embrace School:

Father God wants us to come home and be sons and daughters in an intimate relationship with him. However, we develop our image of God through our image of our earthly fathers. We project our image of our Dad onto God.

If you feel you have had a false image of God or have not seen Him as a servant Father who is humble, loving, and compassionate—you may want to pray for the ungodly belief to be broken.

✞ "Father, I come to you in Jesus' name. I ask you to forgive me for misjudging You for so many years. Please forgive me for distancing myself from You because I did not understand Your true nature of love and humility."

✞ Choose to forgive your parental figures for misrepresenting Father God's love. Pray a blessing over them and for the Father to reveal His love and grace.

✞ Choose to forgive pastors, teachers, churches, or denominations for misrepresenting a loving Father. Now pray a blessing over them and for the Father to reveal His unconditional love to them. They may still be hurting because they do not know the grace and unconditional love of the Father.

✞ Renounce the ungodly belief of Father being an angry God.

✞ Renounce a religious spirit that has sought to earn levels of God's love and acceptance through your human effort or religious striving.

✞ Renounce any sense of shame, guilt, or self condemnation that you may feel because you have never felt good enough to draw close to the Father.

✟ "I choose to receive You as my loving Father. I now see how loving and compassionate you are. I know that I can find rest in Your gentleness and humility. I come home to You and ask You to bring me into You loving arms and reveal the love that You have for me."[92]

FATHER ISSUES

The influence of a father in a child's life is so important that we need to understand how the type of father we have affects the adult characteristics we develop. In addition, the absence of a father will dramatically affect a child psychological by not satisfying his father hunger needs thereby impacting his future adult life. It is therefore important to understand these types of father issues.

Introduction to Father Issues from Shiloh Place Ministries. Experiencing Father's Embrace School:

Often we carry unresolved conflict towards our earthly father or father figures that can hinder us from intimacy with God. Sometimes, there still lies unconscious hidden core pain from our father relationship within our mind, will, our emotions (the soul). Hidden core pain can result from a father's spoken insults, broken promises, outright rejection demeaning looks, disappointments, grief, or abandonment. These FATHER ISSUES can influence our ability to fully trust being intimate with the heavenly Father. Our image of Father God has become shaded by our image of our earthly fathers as we transfer to Father God many of our feelings about our earthly fathers.

How we see Father God determines whether we can receive love, security, acceptance, rest, comfort, provision, and healing in His presence. Even a small flaw in our earthly father's character can distort our ability to receive in Father God's love. These flaws—great and small—create some of our deepest problems in receiving God as a loving Father. No matter how much your earthly father provided for your physical needs, if you did not feel safe, secure, and comforted by his love and his presence, then you may feel Father God is far off.[93]

Your earthly father may fall into one of six basic father type categories, each affecting your image of God in a different way.

1. The Good Father

Physically, the children have a solid roof over their heads, nice clothes to wear, and good food to eat. Emotionally, these fathers are stable and loving, spending time with their children, meeting their needs for security and affirmation, and seeming to do everything a father should... However,...children may become overly attached to their earthly fathers and not develop an intimate relationship with God...They...can find their adult identity only in serving Him rather than being intimate with Him... Daughters may experience difficulty "leaving and cleaving" when the time comes for them to leave their father's home and become a wife to their husband. They may compare their spouse with the unattainable characteristics of their father, with the spouse rarely measuring up.[94]

Events in the father's life may cause changes to his ability to be a provider for the family. Those could be either health issues or employment issues. In 2008, the bad economy of the world caused hundreds of thousands of parents to lose their jobs and their homes. The security of the family unit was being destroyed and it did not take much to establish an argument that the enemy had an influence on the economy to cause this result. One of

Satan's purposes is to destroy the intimacy and security of the family through whatever means possible. Fathers want so much to continue to provide all the things that their children have grown accustomed to, and may continually promise to provide or do for them once things get better. However, children who have experienced this in the past can attest that these broken promises develop into disappointment, rejection, anger, lack of trust, and fear about finances. Children find it difficult to trust God and other people. Spouses are constantly anxious over the state of their finances because of the fear of poverty they experienced in childhood, and lack of intimacy in their relationships.

2. The Performance Oriented Father

"Stringent demands for a child's perfect obedience and high performance standards, if not tempered with large amounts of expressed love, affirmation, and praise, often result in many problems later in life.[95]

The child constantly strives for perfection in order to gain the father's love; however, being human beings, perfection is not attainable. The child is just not good enough to have a place in the father's heart. The wounded child passes forth into an adult relationship with God with a lie that "I only belong and am loved and accepted for what I do and how well I do it."

3. The Passive Father

The passive father makes no great demands on his children, but neither is there any overt rejection. He simply fails to be home even when he is hone. He is not able to demonstrate love or affection, usually not intentionally, because he himself never received these things from his own father. This may even become a generational or a cultural stronghold that is passed down from father to son for centuries. European families generally show very little affection or tenderness; Asian fathers are generally shame based and have very high expectations of successful performance from their children.[96]

Ethnographic research on Chinese culture suggests that it is a *shame socialized culture*. Children are socialized to be conscious of what others think of them and are expected to act so as to get the most out of the approval of others while trying to avoid their disapproval. This begins when Chinese parents shift from being highly indulgent during infancy and toddlerhood to using parenting practices such as scolding, shaming, and physical punishment at the *age of understanding,* which is seen to occur around four to six years of age. Shame is used to teach children right from wrong, and Chinese parents appear to understand that shame should be used only when necessary, because too much shame may harm the child's self esteem (Fung 1999). Observational research by Peggy Miller and her colleagues (Miller; Fung; and Mintz 1996) using small samples of Chinese mothers and children has shown that Chinese mothers' narrative retelling of young children's transgressions focuses on inducing both guilt and shame. This has been found to differ from comparable observational studies of European-American middle class mothers, whose disciplinary practices are more focused on maintaining and enhancing children's self esteem (Wiley et al. 1998). These findings suggest that cultural differences in parenting may be more complex than the simple dichotomy between guilt and shame suggests, and that more research examining parent child interactions in different cultures is needed.[97] The Passive father...does not share his joys, his hopes, his sorrows, or his disappointments with his wife or children. He does not experience life with his family, he simply lives life under the same roof.[98]

4. The Absentee Father

The absentee father is the one who is no longer physically present in the home. This could have been caused by death, divorce, or abandonment.[99]...This can leave you with tremendous hidden core pain of a great void of fatherlessness. You never feel you have a safe place to go to for comfort, security, and affirmation. Over...fifty percent of children in America wake up each morning with someone other than their natural birth father in the home.[100]

This is the category that covers the millions of children during World War II that were orphaned because of the deaths of their fathers or abandonment by occupying soldiers. Many adults in World War II countries continue to search for their biological fathers in order to fill the void in their souls. Children who have had an absentee father may face abandonment issues, and it may be very difficult for them to relate to God. They may fear at some point that when they need God, He won't be there.

5. The Authoritarian Father

These fathers are more interested in the love of law than in the law of love. They go beyond the performance oriented fathers and sternly demand immediate, unquestioned obedience from their children. There is no real emotional relationship that is fostered between the father and the child. The only emotions that seem to be present are intimidation, fear, and control. Children raised in such homes often see God as...the great disciplinarian in the heavens...to be feared and obeyed. They strive to meet His requirements...and end up as servants or slaves to the law instead of intimate sons and daughters...whom the Father loves.[101]

6. The Abusive Father

This is the father that is becoming more common in our present world. These are the verbal, emotional, physical, or sexual abusive fathers in the family relationship. This again is totally against Father God's nature and is not what a father should be...Sexual abuse creates one of the deepest wounds a child could ever receive, for it often results in tremendous hidden core pain.[102]

It affects the trust a child has and all relationships for the rest of that child's life.

However, over the years that I have been a prayer minister, I have seen Jesus through the power of the Holy Spirit gently heal that wounded soul and fill that wound with the Father's love.

Do you have father issues? Our relationship with our earthly father has a direct effect on our relationship with our Heavenly Father. If you did not feel you had a safe, secure, protected place in your father's heart, you may not feel safe anywhere in this earth. You will never, feel safe, secure, and protected in the Heavenly Father's arms. You will spend your life time looking for a place to belong.

Did your father make promises he could not keep? Did your father provide a safe protected home environment for you? Was your father compassionate when you failed? Did you feel love and acceptance all the time or was your acceptance based on your performance? Did your father show you affection by providing a safe place in his arms? Was your father loving and kind to your mother, brothers, and sisters? Did your father provide a special place in his heart specifically for you that no one could take away? Did he hold you, speak tenderly to you, take you up onto his lap, and provide a special time of favor

and intimacy? Did your father meet the financial needs
of the family? Were you worried about food being on the
table, electricity being shut off, or losing your place to live
because your parents lost their jobs and the house? The
mortgage couldn't be paid. Did your father spend quality
time playing with you and nurturing you? Was his voice
tender, did his eyes reflect love? Did you have fun with
your father or were you afraid of your father? Was your
father there for you when you needed him?[103]

The Four Faces of Love

Bob Mumford examines four kinds of love in "Agape Road":

> The Greek language, from which our English New
> Testament was translated, has several words for "love,"
> while the English language has only one. We use the
> same word when we say, "I love God," and, "I love my
> dog," but they certainly do not have the same depth of
> meaning. The Greek words for love are *Storgos, Phileo,
> Agape, and Eros.*
> 1. The essential meaning for *Storgos* or *Astorgos* is
> without love, heartless, or without a family or natural
> affection. It speaks of the hardening and loss of affection
> toward our relatives or relations...Used in a mother-child
> relationship, it implies...that the natural bond a mother
> has for her children has been lost or destroyed. This can
> be seen more prevalently today by...the increase of abor-
> tions to avoid personal inconvenience.[104]

However, depending on the context that the word is
used, it can also refer to familial love or natural affection
such as the love of a parent towards a child.

2. The essential meaning of *Phileo* is "tender affection." It is love that is reciprocal, expressing friendship, trust, and openness. Phileo is friendship moved by qualities inherent in the one loved. The word is used most remarkably of Father and Son in John 3:35 and 5:20. Phileo is essentially reciprocal—I love you because you love me.[105]

3. God is *Agape* (see 1 John 4:16). The essential meaning of *Agape* is an exercise of the divine will in deliberate choice, made without assignable cause, save that which lies in the nature of God Himself (see Deut. 7:7-8). It is God's absolute by which He measures all things (see Acts 17:31). It is used both as a noun and a verb. *Agape* does not love because of beauty or value discovered; it is a love that comes out of His own nature. While Phileo is reciprocal, *Agape* always reveals God's own character. *Agape*, when understood, quickly reveals our need for Christ, who is Agape Incarnate.

Agape unfolds in three progressive steps:
- ♱ *Love God* with all of my heart, soul, mind, and strength (see Mark 12:30).
- ♱ *Love Myself* because God loves me (see Matt. 22:39; Rom. 5:8). He has given me value and worth by pouring His own love into me while I was yet a sinner.
- ♱ *Love Others,* even our enemies, in the same manner and degree that He loved us and gave Himself for us (see Matt. 5:43-48). This is God's love replicated in His own.[106]

4. The essential meaning of *Eros* is the desire or intention to possess, acquire, or control. *Eros* does not seek to be accepted by its object, but to gain possession of it. *Eros* has an appetite or yearning desire that is aroused by the attractive qualities of its object. *Eros*, in Greek philosophy,

came to mean that which is loved for the purpose of personal satisfaction. It is from this posture that the word *Eros* took on its sexual and ultimately pornographic connotation. The word is not primarily sexual, but has more to do with living for my own personal advantage.[107]

Love that has personal reward and self-satisfaction as its motive has the tendency and capacity to annul the *Agape* of God. Self will, that which is self-pleasing, is the negation of love to God...*Eros* is self-referential, causing us to lose the central appeal of Jesus Christ to "take up your cross and follow Me." The loss of *Agape* and its demand for self-renunciation leads us to "cross-less Christianity."...*Eros* is the mother of all sins...It is not only self-centered, but it becomes self-consuming, turning increasingly inward upon itself in a tighter and tighter spiral...The Greek symbol for *Eros* is a serpent consuming its own tail. It is a highly refined form of self-interest and self-seeking. It is a love that has become so distorted that its only purpose is to meet its own needs.[108]

THE MOTHER HEART OF FATHER GOD

The feminine nature of God is that which nurtures, teaches, trains and disciplines.

Introduction to Mother Issues from Shiloh Place Ministries, Experiencing Father's Embrace School:

Many people are hindered in their ability to have healthy loving relationships because of what is transferred to them during the pregnancy of their mothers. As stated before in the story of Moses, we know that wounding in a person's life can start as early as in the womb. The feelings, emotions, and the response to life's experiences that the mother has can be translated to her unborn baby. The problem is that they are not always properly interpreted by the child. All my life I have had problems getting in touch with my emotions. I thought that it might be related to storge love deprivation. However, I recently requested an inner healing ministry session to address this issue. To my amazement, God revealed that my emotional condition was the result of the feelings and emotions I received from my mother while in the womb. It was the beginning of 1945. Friends, relatives, and my dad were in the war. People were dying and the hardship, pain, and emotions were unbearable. My prayer minister and I discussed the possibility that people during this time may have become numb to their emotions on purpose. That my mother made a vow that she would not allow herself to feel the pain, to shut down her emotions so that if my dad was killed, it would not hurt so much. That was when I received confirmation from the Father that this was the truth, as I experienced His love, peace, and joy flow through me starting at the top of my head and slowly ending at my toes. The truth had been revealed and the lie was now broken. As an unborn baby I had interpreted that held-in emotions were to be normal during life.

Many people are also hindered in their ability to have healthy loving relationships because they did not receive the right kind of love from their mothers in their formative years. On an annulment questionnaire, the very first question is, "What did you learn about love from your parents."

Mother's are the primary caregivers and dispensers of *storge* love in the child's first two years of life. *Storge* love is from the Greek word "*storge*" which means "natural affection," like that felt by parents for offspring. It is almost always use as a descriptor of relationships within the family. The father's primary years of influence are the third through the fifth year.

Storge love is demonstrated in three primary ways by mothers:

1. **Affectionate Touch.** Doctors have scientifically proven that without a regular daily dose of affectionate touch the body and the emotions become unhealthy."[109]

It is a basic need for every human being to receive affirmation during childhood development. Every child needs to feel that it is loved. During World War II, the babies in England's orphanages started to show signs of unusual physical development. The caretakers changed them, feed them, and bathed them, but no one was holding them. The heads of these babies continued to grow while their bodies did not. The babies began to die. These babies literally were starving for love. Then young women from the countryside were brought in to hold the babies and nurture them with love. When they did, the babies began to grow. The basic need for love and affirmation was met. This condition was later named Marasmus.

A Dutch psychiatrist, Dr. Anna A. Terruwe, discovered Emotional Deprivation Disorder in the 1960s, and it was called the Frustration Neurosis or Deprivation Neurosis when translated into the English language by her colleague, Dr. Conrad W. Baars. EDD is described by the authors as follows:

A person is unaffirmed when he or she has been deprived of authentic affirmation. He or she may have been criticized, ignored, neglected, abused, or emotionally rejected by primary caregivers early in life, resulting in the individual's stunted emotional growth. Unaffirmed individuals are incapable of developing into emotionally mature adults without receiving authentic affirmation from another person. Maturity is reached when there is a harmonious relationship between a person's body, mind, emotions, and spiritual soul under the guidance of their reason and will.

EDD individuals are described as "incapable of establishing normal, mature contact with others. This abnormal emotional rapport with others causes the person to feel lonely and uncomfortable in social settings he or she feels like a stranger, not part of the group."[110]

The term "anaclitic depression" was coined and promoted by psychiatrist and psychoanalyst René Spitz. Its first significant mention was in Spitz's article on "Hospitalism" (1945). The kindred concepts of hospitalism and anaclitic depression are described in chapter 14 of *The First Year of Life* (Spitz and Cobliner, 1965). For Spitz, such depressions are attributable to emotional deficiency.[111]

Anaclitic depression is the impairment of an infant's physical, social, and intellectual development following separation from its mother or primary caregiver. It is also known as a syndrome occurring in infants, usually after sudden separation from the mothering person. Symptoms include apprehension, withdrawal, detachment, incessant crying, refusal to eat, sleep disturbances, and eventually, stupor leading to severe impairment of the infant's physical, social, and intellectual development. If the mothering figure or a substitute is made available within 1 to 3 months, the infant recovers quickly with no long term effects.

Recently I met Freddie Tuyizere who is in charge of the youth ministry in Burundi. We discussed the children who have witnessed their fathers being killed, mothers raped and killed, and their sisters taken away for prostitution.

They do not feel anyone loves them. They cannot understand how our God could possibly love them. Some of these children have stopped growing. Freddie said that he has met children, who finally understand the Love of the Father, no longer stare without emotion, but smile, and start growing again. This is happening today in the year 2009.[112]

There is another story in Jack Winter's book, "The Home Coming," of a boy who was born to parents that wanted a girl so they wanted nothing to do with him. He was fed with a propped up bottle, was rarely held or spoken to, and spent most of his time lying flat on his back in a crib. As he grew, bottles of lukewarm milk and fruit juice were placed at the end of the bed for him to pick up and feed himself. At the time he was placed into foster care, he was a chubby ball; his eyes were big and brown, but unresponsive. His head, which was totally out of proportion to the rest of his body, was flat on the back. He was unable to sit up even when assisted and seemed to be locked into a world of his own. The foster parents poured themselves into this little guy and he soaked up all the love his heart could hold. As he began to bond with them and trust them to care for him, he slowly gained control over his body and the world around him. He even became a straight A student in high school.

2. **Eye Contact:** The eyes are the windows of the soul where love is communicated to a child (Luke 11:34 NASB). The eye is the lamp of your body; when your eye is clear, your whole body also is full of light; but when it is bad, your body also is full of darkness. If children don't see understanding, loving looks in the eyes of their parents, it can leave a wound that remains unhealed all through life.

3. **Tone of voice:** Loving tones nurture the soul and help children feel acceptance and value so they can walk free from the fear of rejection and failure. When a mother picks up her baby, love, comfort and tenderness begin to flow through her to that child. The baby senses that she is doing everything possible to meet their needs. She is demonstrating *storge* love.

Lack of storge love leads to unhealthy Eros love during puberty. Eros is the Greek word for physical and sexual attraction. Those who do not receive healthy amounts of storge as a child may have unhealthy sexual drives, urges, compulsions, addictions, and uncontrollable fantasies. A person may have the inability to established nonsexual relationships based on the love for that person instead of the lust for that person. This may have devastating effects on a person's future relationships and can lead to other problems throughout their lifetime.

As adults, they try to get their unhealed need met through eros and sex. It often results in pornography and masturbation addiction, but they are really searching for intimacy, nurture, and comfort that were lost.

If we are uncomfortable with ourselves, we are uncomfortable with others and with God. We may stop liking ourselves and begin to believe we have no value. Until our need for storge love is met we are vulnerable to sexual temptation. We often lack the ability to care about others' needs. We lack the ability to be intimate and caring. We lack empathy and compassion and value people for what they can do for us. This carries over in our relationships with God as we value what He can do for us, but we have no concept of what intimacy and love is all about. They have a deep void that they can never satisfy. It can lead to a cycle of woundedness that may end in feelings of despair and that life is too painful to live. *"I just wish Jesus would come back and take me home."*¹¹³

I can't tell you how many times I have said the same thing to myself and other people in my lifetime. People would look at me as if I were crazy. My favorite saying was, "Why on earth would I want to stay here in this hell we live in when I can be happy being with Jesus?" All my life people would ask me, "Why don't you ever smile? You don't seem to be a happy person." I never had an answer. I don't remember my mother ever hugging me and telling me she loved me. My aunts swear that my mother loved me. However, I discovered I had all the symptoms of storge love depravation, which was hidden to my consciousness. I was uncomfortable with myself and therefore uncomfortable with others. I stopped liking myself. I lacked the ability to care about others' needs. I lacked the ability to be intimate and caring. I lacked empathy and compassion and valued people for what they could do for me. This carried over into my relationship with God as I valued what He could do for me, but I had no concept of what intimacy and love was all about. I needed healing for the lack of storge love that I didn't know was lacking in my childhood. Where there is fruit, there is a root.

Healing for Lack of Storge Love

1. Realize that no human being can fully meet our need for storge love.

It is difficult to teach someone how to love until he has experienced it. Love and intimacy have been programmed into your genetic code. In Christ, God has placed his DNA. Christ is in you, he abides in you. You are created in God's image (Love). You cannot help but conform to your Father's attributes! Everything God has created within you has naturally been created for intimate, loving relationships, but you cannot have healthy relationships with others until your need for love has been met in Him.

2. Realize that you were not a victim of the lack of storge love.

Even if you were physically or emotionally wounded as a child, do not take on a victim mentality and believe that you have never been loved. IT IS A LIE. You have never been alone or without love. God has constantly pursued you with love and comfort. No matter what your mother's circumstances were, you were not an intrusion.

3. Be willing to let go of counterfeit affections and false loves.

Perhaps you never received storge love from your mother, and the deep longing that has been left in your heart has influenced you to seek wrong answers for right needs. When you allow God to meet your need for nurture and comfort, you no longer need the false loves anymore. Your mother may have been so wounded that she was not able to be there for you in your times of need, but God has never abandoned or forsaken you. He is not ashamed of you. He will pour storge love into the barren areas of your soul.

4. Realize that Father God's Mother Heart wants to bond to you and meet your deepest needs for storge love.

In God's nature there is a mother's heart—the storge love that comforts us in the tenderness and compassion and nurture. God created a woman "in his own image" (Genesis 1:27).[114]

And He made from one man every nation of mankind to live on all the face of the earth, having determined their appointed times and the boundaries of their habitation. He determined the exact time and the exact location you were to be born. You are here on purpose and for a purpose. (Jeremiah 1:5)[115] "Before I formed you in the womb I knew you, And before you were born I consecrated you; I have appointed you a prophet to the nations." (Acts 17:26 NASB)[116]

On his "Foundations of the Father's Love" CD, Reverend Harold Martin teaches that:

Before your parents ever thought about you, God had formed you in his mind. It didn't matter where you were conceived or how you were conceived, you are not a mistake. Your parents were the elements He used to get you here. You were not an accident.

The mother and father that you grew up with are not the mother and father that God wanted for you. He didn't create your parents wounded, he didn't create your parents to be harsh or angry, He created them in His love with the thought in mind that there would never be a moment in time that you would not see love in your mother and father's eyes. That you would not hear love and acceptance in their voices. That there would never be a time in your life that perfect love and acceptance didn't flow through to you. That you always feel love, comfort, and security. That was God's plan for them and that was God's plan for you.

What happened to the plan? It was the inequities of the forefathers that were passed down to the third and fourth generation that brought about wounding to the parents. It was the sins of others against them, in their youth that destroyed their ability to receive love. God created your parents to be a perfect reflection of His love for you.

When you think about what your parents went through, about what they suffered, the wounding that they went through, then it is amazing that they were as good parents as they were. Wounded people wound people. Hurt people hurt people.[117]

How does God see us?

God sings! Think of it, the great Jehovah or Yahweh, singing! Can we really believe it? Is it possible to conceive of Deity breaking into song: Father, Son and Holy Spirit together, singing over the redeemed? God is so happy in the love which He gives to His people that He breaks His eternal silence, and sun and moon and stars are astonished to hear God chanting a hymn of joy.

The lord will take great delight in you,
He will quiet you with his love,
He will rejoice over you with singing
(Zephaniah 3:17)

Three things are said here about the way the Father views those who are adopted as his sons and daughters. First, the Father takes great delight in us…Second, it says that he will quiet us with his love. The Father woos us into a place of security and serenity by revealing the depth of his love for us…Thirdly—and most wonderful of all—it says that the Father rejoices over us with singing.[118]

We are His happy thoughts. "For the Father himself loves you, because you have loved Me, and have believed that I came forth from the Father." (John 16:27). Because of Adam and Eve, and also because of our own sin nature we were born into the slavery of sin. This was the result of our orphan heart, orphan spirit, and spiritual orphan mentality. However, His heart longed for us to again have a close intimate relationship with Him. "For God so loved the world, that he sent his only begotten son" (John 3:16). "I will not leave you as orphans; I will come to you." (John 14:18). All he wants is for you to crawl up into his lap so that you can experience how much He loves you. Father God opened the door for the spirit of Adoption back to His heart through Christ.

Barry Adams has put together a number of God's words into "The Father's Love Letter."

THE FATHER'S LOVE LETTER

My Child

You may not know me, but I know everything about you
~Psalm 139:1

I know when you sit down and when you rise up
~Psalm 139:2

I am familiar with all your ways ~Psalm 139:3

Even the very hairs on your head are numbered
~Matthew 10:29-31

For you were made in my image ~Genesis 1:27

In me you live and move and have your being
~Acts 17:28

For you are my offspring ~Acts 17:28

I knew you even before you were conceived
~Jeremiah 1:4-5

I chose you when I planned creation
~Ephesians 1:11 12

You were not a mistake, for all your days are written in
my book ~Psalm 139:15-16

I determined the exact time of your birth and where
you would live ~Acts 17:26

You are fearfully and wonderfully made ~Psalm 139:14

I knit you together in your mother's womb
~Psalm 139:13

And brought you forth on the day you were born
~Psalm 71:6

I have been misrepresented by those who don't know me
~John 8:41-44

I am not distant and angry, but am the complete
expression of love ∞1 John 4:16

And it is my desire to lavish my love on you ∞1 John 3:1

Simply because you are my child and I am your father
∞1 John 3:1

I offer you more than your earthly father ever could
∞Matthew 7:11

For I am the perfect father ∞Matthew 5:48

Every good gift that you receive comes from my hand
∞James 1:17

For I am your provider and I meet all your needs
∞Matthew 6:31 33

My plan for your future has always been filled with hope
∞Jeremiah 29:11

Because I love you with an everlasting love
∞Jeremiah 31:3

My thoughts toward you are countless as the sand on
the seashore ∞Psalm 139:17-18

And I rejoice over you with singing ∞Zephaniah 3:17

I will never stop doing good to you ∞Jeremiah 32:40

For you are my treasured possession ∞Exodus 19:5

I desire to establish you with all my heart and all my soul
∞Jeremiah 32:41

And I want to show you great and marvelous things
∞Jeremiah 33:3

If you seek me with all your heart, you will find me
∞Deuteronomy 4:29

Delight in me and I will give you the desires of your heart
∞Psalm 37:4

For it is I who gave you those desires ∞Philippians 2:13

I am able to do more for you than you could possibly
imagine ∞Ephesians 3:20

For I am your greatest encourager
 ❧2 Thessalonians 2:16-17

I am also the Father who comforts you in all your troubles
 ❧2 Corinthians 1:3-4

When you are brokenhearted, I am close to you
 ❧Psalm 34:18

As a shepherd carries a lamb, I have carried you close
to my heart ❧Isaiah 40:11

One day I will wipe away every tear from your eyes
 ❧Revelation 21:3-4

And I'll take away all the pain you have suffered on
this earth ❧Revelation 21:3-4

I am your Father, and I love you even as I love my son,
Jesus ❧John 17:23

For in Jesus, my love for you is revealed ❧John 17:26

He is the exact representation of my being
 ❧Hebrews 1:3

He came to demonstrate that I am for you, not against
you ❧Romans 8:31

And to tell you that I am not counting your sins
 ❧2 Corinthians 5:18-19

Jesus died so that you and I could be reconciled
 ❧2 Corinthians 5:18-19

His death was the ultimate expression of my love for you
 ❧1 John 4:10

I gave up everything I loved that I might gain your love
 ❧Romans 8:31-32

If you receive the gift of my son Jesus, you receive me
 ❧1 John 2:23

And nothing will ever separate you from my love again
 ❧Romans 8:38-39

Come home and I'll throw the biggest party heaven has
ever seen ❧Luke 15:7

I have always been Father, and will always be Father
    ↝Ephesians 3:14-15

My question is: Will you be my child? ↝John 1:12-13

I am waiting for you ↝Luke 15:11-32

Love, Your Dad, Almighty God

Chapter Seven

From Orphans to Sonship

ADOPTION

There is a place for you in Dad's house. That is where I am, and I am getting your place ready. I will not leave you an orphan but will come to you, and the Father and I will make our home in you. *(See John 14:18,23).*

In Roman adoption, the father is the one who chooses to adopt. In spiritual adoption the Father chooses to adopt you. *But you have received the spirit of adoption* (Rom. 8:15, c.f. Gal. 4:5).[119] In Roman adoption they adopted a slave. We were slaves to sin or to the father of lies, but then we got adopted into a new family where Jesus brought us back home again to where we belong; to be part of the family again where there is love, where there is security, where there is value, and where there is purpose. A Roman father paid fees for son he adopted. St. Paul understood the Roman adoption process when he talks about adoption. You were adopted and Father God paid for you with His son's precious blood, so you could belong to His family and become adopted as a son or daughter of a loving Father. The story is all about the loving Father, not the prodigal son or the older son. In Roman society adoption, could not be reversed.

The ancient Roman adoption process
According to William Barclay, the Roman adoption process that was utilized during the time of the Apostles is what St. Paul alludes to in his letters to the Romans.

> For you have not received a spirit of slavery leading to fear again, but you have received a spirit of adoption as sons by which we cry out, "Abba! Father!" The Spirit Himself testifies with our spirit that we are children of God, and if children, heirs also, heirs of God and fellow heirs with Christ, if indeed we suffer with Him so that we may also be glorified with Him. For the anxious longing of the creation waits eagerly for the revealing of the sons of God *(Romans 8:15 17,19)*.

Roman adoption demonstrated the father's power over the family. A Roman son never came of age, no matter how old he was. He was still the father's absolute possession and under his absolute control. However, in order to be adopted into another family, there had to occur a symbolic sale. Three times this symbolism of sale was carried out. Twice the father sold his son and then would buy him back. The third time he would not buy him back. There followed a ceremony in which the adopting father would go to a Roman magistrate and present a legal case for the transference of the son to be adopted. This completed the adoption. It is this process that was in St. Paul had in mind when he wrote to the Romans. There were consequences of the adoption process. The adopted person lost all rights from his old family, but now had the right of a legitimate son in the new family. He became an heir to his new father's estate. His old life was completely wiped out such as debts.

> The *patria potestas* was the father's power over his family; that power was absolute; it was actually the power of absolute disposal and control, and in the early days it was actually the power of life and death. In regard to his father, a Roman son never came of age. No matter how old he was, he was still under the *patria potestas*, in the absolute possession, and under the absolute control, of his father. Obviously this made adoption into another family very difficult and a very serious step.
>
> In adoption a person had to pass from one *patria potestas* to another. He had to pass out of the possession and control of one father into the equally absolute control and possession of another. There were two steps. The first was known as *mancipatio*, and it was carried out by a symbolic sale, in which copper and scales were symbolically used. Three times the symbolism of sale was carried out. Twice the father symbolically sold his son, and twice he bought him back; and the third time he did not buy him back and thus the *patria potestas* was held to be broken.
>
> After the sale there followed a ceremony called vindication. The adopting father went to the praetor, one of the Roman magistrates, and presented a legal case for the transference of the person to be adopted into his *patria potestas*. When all this was completed the adoption was complete. Clearly this was a serious and impressive step.[120]

This is the example that Paul uses when he speaks of the glory of adoption into the family of God:

Proverbs 23:7 says that we become according to what we think in our hearts. If you think like an orphan, you will live like an orphan. If you think you do not have a home, you will live life as if you do not have a home. If you think like a son, you will live like a son. If you think you have a home, you will live life as if you have a home.[121]

SONSHIP

This urban legend first appeared on the internet in 2002. It is attributed to Dr Fred Craddock who is seminary professor of homiletics at Emory University in Atlanta However, the actual origin is still unknown.

A seminary professor was vacationing with his wife in Gatlinburg, Tennessee. One morning, they were eating breakfast at a little restaurant, hoping to enjoy a quiet, family meal. While they were waiting for their food, they noticed a distinguished looking, white-haired man moving from table to table, visiting with the guests. The professor leaned over and whispered to his wife, "I hope he doesn't come over here."

But sure enough, the man did come over to their table. "Where are you folks from?" he asked in a friendly voice. "Oklahoma," they answered. "Great to have you here in Tennessee," the stranger said. "What do you do for a living?" "I teach at a seminary," he replied. "Oh, so you teach preachers how to preach, do you? Well, I've got a really great story for you." And with that, the gentleman pulled up a chair and sat down at the table with the couple.

The professor groaned and thought to himself, "'Great. Just what I need...another preacher story!" The man started, "See that mountain over there?" (pointing out the restaurant window). Not far from the base of that mountain, there was a boy born to an unwed mother. He had a hard time growing up, because every place he went, he was always asked the same question, "Hey boy, who's your Daddy?" Whether he was at school, in the grocery store, or drug store, people would ask the same question, "Who's your daddy?"

He would hide at recess and lunchtime from other students. He would avoid going into stores because that question hurt him so bad. When he was about 12 years old, a new preacher came to his church. He would always go in late and slip out early to avoid hearing the question, "Who's your daddy?"

But one day, the new preacher said the benediction so fast that he got caught and had to walk out with the crowd. Just about the time he got to the back door, the new preacher, not knowing anything about him, put his hand on his shoulder and asked him, "Son, who's your daddy?"

The whole church got deathly quiet. He could feel every eye in the church looking at him. Now everyone would finally know the answer to the question, "Who's your daddy?"

This new preacher, though, sensed the situation around him and using discernment that only the Holy Spirit could give, said the following to that scared little boy. "Wait a minute! I know who you are! I see the family resemblance now. You are a child of God."

With that he patted the boy on his shoulder and said, "Boy, you've got a great inheritance. Go and claim it." With that, the boy smiled for the first time in a long time and walked out the door a changed person. He was never the same again. Whenever anybody asked him, "Who's your Daddy?"' he'd just tell them, "I'm a Child of God."

The distinguished gentleman got up from the table and said, "Isn't that a great story?" The professor responded that it really was a great story! As the man turned to leave, he said, "You know, if that new preacher hadn't told me that I was one of God's children, I probably never would have amounted to anything!" And then he walked away.

The seminary professor and his wife were stunned. He called the waitress over and asked her, "Do you know who that man was the one who just left that was sitting at our table?'" The waitress grinned and said, "Of course. Everybody here knows him. That's Ben Hooper. He's the former governor of Tennessee!'"[122]

> The Greek word for sonship is *huiothesia* meaning "adoption." Here is the NIV translation of Galatians 4:5 6: "But when the time had come, God sent his Son, born of a woman, born under law, to redeem those under law, that we might receive the full rights of sons." The phrase "full rights of sons" is a translation of *huiothesia,* which most recent researchers insist should be translated "'adoption."[123]

Before Christ, we believed we were servants of God. Jesus was transitioning his disciples from orphan mentality, thinking like servants, into being able to think like sons. Thinking like sons was a huge paradigm shift that was 180 degrees from the first paradigm shift with Adam and Eve. It is one the church is still working on to this day.

> Many believers never move on from an image of God as a punitive judge and not a loving father... The net result of this is that believers start to live a life of legalism rather than a life of love... If we are to be set free we must move from a place where we fear God to a place where we can love Him as well. For this to occur, we must allow the Holy Spirit to flood our hearts with the revelation of God as "Abba Father." We need the loving spirit of adoption to penetrate the deepest places of our lives and to bring about a divine disclosure of the true nature of God. We need to move from slavery to sonship.[124]

Paul refers to adoption in five different letters.

But when the time had fully come, God sent his Son, born of a woman, born under the law, to redeem those under law, that we might receive adoption *(Galatians 4:4-5).*

In love God predestined us to be adopted as his sons through Jesus Christ, in accordance with pleasure and will *(Ephesians 1:5).*

For you did not receive a spirit that makes you a slave again to fear, but you received the Spirit of adoption. And by him we cry, "Abba Father" *(Romans 8:15).*

We ourselves, who have the first fruits of the spirit, groan inwardly as we wait eagerly for our adoption, the redemption of our bodies *(Romans 8:23).*

Theirs is the adoption as sons; theirs the divine glory, the covenants, the receiving of the law, the temple worship and the promises *(Romans 9:4).*

Before you and I became believers, we were living as orphans and slaves. We did not know God as our Father. We were under the *patria potestas* of Satan, the father of lies. We were weighed down by the heavy debt of sin and consequently separate from Christ, excluded from citizenship in Israel and foreigners to the covenants of the promise, without hope and without God in the world (Ephesians 2:12).

If we want to become God's sons and daughters, we must therefore believe that Jesus paid the adoption price on the cross, that he died to set us free from sin, and accept him as our Savior and Lord. When we make that decision, we break through the sin barrier with saving faith as opposed to good works. The cross is therefore the bridge over which we must travel if we want to be delivered from slavery into sonship.[125]

If we're honest, though, our image of God is colored by our own fathers. Those who have had absent or cruel fathers tend to find it hard to believe in the perfection of God's fatherly love.[126]

The image of God as in Ephesians
(Ephesians 1:3-13)

The eternal plan of the father

Blessed <u>be</u> the God and Father of our Lord Jesus Christ, who has blessed us with every spiritual blessing in the heavenly places in Christ, just as He chose us in Him before the foundation of the world, that we would be holy and blameless before Him. In love He predestined us to adoption as sons through Jesus Christ to Himself, according to the kind intention of His will, to the praise of the glory of His grace, which He freely bestowed on us in the Beloved.

Fulfillment through Christ

In Him we have redemption through His blood, the forgiveness of our trespasses, according to the riches of His grace which He lavished on us. In all wisdom and insight He made known to us the mystery of His will, according to His kind intention which He purposed in Him with a view to an administration suitable to the fullness of the times, that is, the summing up of all things in Christ, things in the heavens and things on the earth.

Inheritance through the Spirit

In Him also we have obtained an inheritance, having been predestined according to His purpose who works all things after the counsel of His will, to the end that we who were the first to hope in Christ would be to the praise of His glory. In Him, you also, after listening to the message of truth, the gospel of your salvation—having also believed, you were sealed in Him with the Holy Spirit of promise.[127]

THE SPIRIT OF ADOPTION

In "From Orphans to Heirs" Mark Stibbe continues his analysis of spiritual adoption:

One of Satan's major strategies is to prevent believers from enjoying the glorious freedom of the children of God. He works tirelessly to deceive us that we have to earn the Father's acceptance through legalism. Many people become trapped by this deception, and they start to become burnt out. God seems further and further away. Christian ministry becomes an arduous duty rather than a constant joy. When this happens we become oppressed by a spirit of slavery and fear. Far from being led by the Spirit into deeper and deeper intimacy with the Father, we are driven by the flesh into greater and greatest exhaustion. Instead of being drawn into sweeter communion with Abba, Father, we are driven by legalism into a lifeless, religious emptiness.[128]

The two sons in the story told in Luke 15 demonstrate the two forms of spiritual slavery, hedonism, and legalism. The first son lives as a slave to sin in the distant country where he squanders his father's wealth. The second son lives as a slave to law in his own country as he slaves away for his father, obeying every order given to him. In a sense, both are unworthy to be called the father's sons. Yet the father chooses to address both of them as his sons, thereby wooing them towards that place where they no longer have to strive for or against his affections, but simply rest and rejoice in the knowledge that their father loves them...

It is easy to forget that there is a third son in Luke 15:11-32, the Son who is actually telling the story. While the two sons in the story model the kinds of spiritual slavery from which we need rescuing, the Son actually telling the story represents the state which we are called to receive, namely, sonship. Both boys in the story could live as sons, but both choose to live as slaves. Meanwhile, the one telling the tale stands outside the story modeling what true sonship really entails.

Romans 6 describes slavery to sin, Romans 7 describes slavery to the law. Romans 8 describes the state of sonship. In Romans 8 we learn that the son is someone who knows that he is accepted by the Father.[129]

Slavery to the law

How does a person become a slave to the law? When his image of God is dysfunctional and warped. When a person sees God as a hard taskmaster or as a punitive slave driver, he has become a slave to the law. When a person doesn't recognize that he does not need to earn God's acceptance, that person has become a slave to the law... When a person fears a distant God, he is in a state of servitude not liberty, misery not joy, insecurity not security... His spirituality is one of religion not relationship. This is the religion of the older brother in the parable of Luke 15.[130]

The legal man always strives to earn Father's approval through good works. His life is dominated by the satanic lie that God only accepts those who slave away for him through strict observance of the law. Preoccupied as he is with appearances, he puts on a mask that disguises the real condition of his heart and invests much in pious, external gestures. He daily applies spiritual cosmetics in order to put on and maintain his face. His walk with God is frenetic, mechanical, and lifeless. He is completely performance oriented driven. His identity is wholly tied up with his achievements and with the approval of others around him. He is a perfectionist and as such, is highly judgmental of everyone else except himself. He points the finger at others and induces guilt in those he condemns. He is cold rather than warm in his relationships and relishes status and control. He is into power games and one-upmanship. He is a slave to *ought* and *must*.[131]

Fear, from a lively sense of the wrath of God, and of the consequences of his wrath; of the punishment which he has justly deserved, and which he sees hanging over his head; fear of death, as being to him the gate of hell, the entrance of death eternal; fear of the devil, the executioner of the wrath and righteous vengeance of God; fear of men... (quoted from John Wesley's sermons[132])

In essence, this fear is a fear of rejection—rejection by God (before and after death), and rejection by others... The only way to set a man free from legalism is through a revelation of the Father heart of God. That is why the father of the prodigal son reveals his heart to his oldest child. He begins with the word, "Son" (literally, "my child"). In these two words he reveals his desire that the older child should live in a Father son rather than a Master servant relationship with him. These are simple words of acceptance and affection. He continues, "You are always with me, and everything I have is yours"[133]

> But while he was still a long way off, his father saw him and was filled with compassion for him; he ran to his son, threw his arms around him, and kissed him *(Luke 15:20)*.

First, we learn the Father is patient... Second, he is a compassionate father... Third, he is a demonstrative father... He cannot help but run towards him, throw his arms around him, and kiss him.[134]

Through the cross, we have been delivered from slavery to sonship. As in the old Roman rite of adoption, we have been bought out of the slave driving influence of our original father (devil) and placed under the loving affection of our new Father in heaven. This act of redemption and emancipation has been purchased not through gold or silver but through the precious blood of Jesus Christ, the Son who became a slave. Through the power of the cross, we have been made sons and daughters of our Father in heaven. We have been delivered from the curse of legalism and liberated from the spirit of slavery. Now we have a new father, a new family, a new home, and a new name.

Through faith in Jesus we become sons and daughters of God (Galatians 3:26)... *But because we are sons and daughters, God sends the Spirit of adoption into our hearts.* The Holy Spirit brings us into the subjective realization of what has been objectively achieved on the cross namely an intimate, heartfelt relationship with God the father... Thus Paul says to the Galatians that they should no longer be driven by the flesh but by the Holy Spirit.

There are many genuinely "born again" people who have been deceived by Satan into believing that they have to earn God's acceptance through exhausting labors and visible successes.[135]

This is called performance-driven Christianity.

Healing the Orphan Heart

Healing is a journey with the Father that has a beginning but continues for a lifetime. Progress in this journey is a process in the Father's love. As long as you have progress, the process is working.

In the following tale, Judith MacNutt examines the three links in the chain of emotional bondage.

The Elephant Story

A man is going through a circus and there is this big elephant. It is bound by a very small chain. And he is with the animal trainer and he said to the trainer, "I have always wanted to ask, how does that chain hold such a large animal?" The trainer said, "It doesn't, but the elephant doesn't know that." He said, "Well I don't understand." The trainer said, "When the elephant is born, we take that same chain and put it on his ankle. It is strong enough then to hold him because he is a baby. As he grows, we continue to use the same chain. Now he is an adult male elephant, which is much stronger than that chain. It is not the chain that binds him; it is the memory of that chain." That is the way inner healing is. Memories keep us in bondage. Memories are crucial in the way we perceive ourselves from our childhood experiences. Especially from the input of our parents. They also affect the choices we make in our lives especially in relationships and careers.

Our own personal emotional bondage will prevent us from having the full emotionally free relationship with God that He desires. There are three links in the chain of emotional bondage. We must be healed in all three areas if we are to become emotionally free.

If you are suffering with a chemical imbalance mood disorder (the first link), it will be very hard to pray, worship, read the Bible, or stop worrying. When one is bombarded with depressing thoughts, it will be very difficult to relax in God's arms of love and enjoy a relationship with Him, or anyone else for that matter. If you have an untreated mood disorder, you will have great difficulty coming to emotional freedom. Please go and get treated before going through with any inner healing steps.

The second link is the direct harassment by Satan. He loves to attack, discourage, distract, and take advantage of our emotional bondage. He will exploit every chemical imbalance and unhealed area of our personality or old nature by filling our minds with lies so we still find it very difficult to receive the love that God so willingly offers us. What we believe to be true is true, even if it is a lie. Know your authority and use it.

The third link is of course comprised of the wounds of our soul or personality. These are the biggest chains that block us from a full relationship with God. All humans have been wounded through damaging relationships with other wounded humans. Wounded people wound people. As we have more and more unsuccessful relationships, we begin to expect failure. This expectation is projected onto God, so we then presume that He will hurt and reject us like everyone else. Satan uses this to distract us from God and he uses the lies he implants to mold us into his image. In this way Satan disrupts our relationships with God, others, and ourselves, which are the three most vital relationships. God wants to heal those wounds and restore our relationships"[136]

Through my research and also my training as a prayer minister, I have come across numerous writings about the importance of forgiveness in the process of healing ministry. None have ever explained it as well as Rodney Hogue, Pastor of Community of Grace Church in Hayward, California, and a frequent speaker at Global Awakening Conferences. It is because his book is used as a tool to help facilitate the healing and restoration of the soul and because of its simplistic presentation that I feel compelled to include excerpts of it here.

FORGIVENESS
By Rodney Hogue

Forgiveness begins by admitting you have been offended. At this point you start with acknowledging the offense. You cannot quickly rid yourself of the offense until you bring it to the surface and call it for what it is. Forgiveness doesn't remove or delete offenses from our lives. Forgiveness doesn't mean that you go into denial and forget this ever happened to you. Forgiveness will not erase your memory clean. What forgiveness does is to remove the power of that memory over your life.

Forgiveness doesn't declare that what the offenders did is now OK. Instead, forgiveness takes an offense seriously, without trying to pass it off as an insignificant and trivial matter. Every wrong produces an indebtedness that we feel. Have you ever heard someone say, "You owe me an apology!"? If I offend you, then I have created a debt and am obligated to pay it. Forgiveness means that you must release what you are owed and not give your offenders what they deserve. Forgiveness acknowledges the debt but you are choosing to cancel it. This is the essence of forgiveness—releasing the other person's indebtedness to you.

Forgiveness means that you are releasing the offender into the care of Jesus who is our just Judge and our Defender. *Never take your own revenge, beloved, but leave room for the wrath of God, for it is written, "Vengeance is Mine, I will repay," says the Lord* (Romans 12:19).

When we hang on to the offense and refuse to release it, we are deciding that we want to stand in God's place and take our own revenge rather than let our Just Judge do it. Genuine forgiveness recognizes that we do not have the right to become the enforcers of justice. To render justice to the offender, it would have to pass through us first since we are standing between God and the offender. Having bound ourselves to our offender through retaining the offense and standing in God's role in seeking to render our own revenge, we position ourselves right in the middle of God's line of sight standing between Him and the offender. For God to have access to the offender to bring about justice, we must release the offender and the offense out of our hands and into the hands of God, our perfect and holy Judge.

One reason you may not want to forgive is because you fear having to reconcile with the other person. However, forgiving a person doesn't mean that reconciliation is the inevitable next step. While forgiveness is always necessary, reconciliation is not. Sometimes reconciliation is impossible because the offender is dead or unreachable. In addition, your offender may not even have any desire to be reconciled. Forgiveness depends on the offended releasing the debt of the offender irregardless of whether the relationship is restored. The offender could be a person who sexually molested you, a person who verbally belittled you, one who physically abused you, or one who betrayed you. If you have been wounded and the potential of further wounding is possible or even probable, safe boundaries are necessary.

Here's the clincher. Your offender still has power over you until you forgive. That ought to irritate you if nothing else. You could be sitting around, angry as you can be, thinking that as long as you do not forgive, you are punishing your offender(s), while in the meantime your offenders can be going about activities of their daily routine enjoying themselves, not even thinking about you, much less concerned about you, and going on with life. *But NO! You are punishing them, right?* Who really is getting punished?

The result of forgiveness is the freedom to pursue the purposes of God for your life. Unforgiveness stifles God's destiny for our lives. It clouds our motives. It pollutes our purpose. It tempts us to deviate from our course. When unforgiveness is present, we find ourselves weighed down and easily worn out. When we have a heart that is willing to forgive, then the weights that hinder us are gone.

You can identify the seed of what you have been sowing by examining the fruit of the crop you are harvesting, both good and bad. Whatever we give out, whether good or bad, will be given back to us in greater portions. That is the law of the harvest. We reap back what we sow, we reap later than we sow, and we reap more than what we sow. So, we have a choice in what we reap; the effects of blessing or the effects of cursing. When we suffer the effect of a curse, the suffering is essentially the damage and ruin toward ourselves for not choosing to give what we have received.

We can receive mercy without giving it. We can receive God's forgiveness of sins without forgiving others who have sinned against us. When we do not give, we shut off the flow of grace from our lives. As a result, spiritual, emotional, and possibly even physical diseases are given permission to operate in us. Another thing that happens when we refuse to forgive is that we are cursing ourselves.

Our tongue can bring blessing or it can bring cursing. Whatever we send forth from our tongue is what we reap. Whatever we send forth with our words returns to us. That is why we are told to "bless our enemies" and "bless those who curse you." James 3:8-10 says, *"But no one can tame the tongue; it is a restless evil and full of deadly poison. With it we bless our Lord and Father; and with it we curse men, who have been made in the likeness of God; from the same mouth came both blessing and cursing. My brethren, these things ought not to be this way."*

When people have not forgiven their parents for wounding they received earlier in life, they cut themselves off emotionally from their parents, often vowing never again to relate to them or be like them. The effect is that you cut off your inheritance. Your parents, regardless of whether they were good or bad, have a source of **blessing** that is your rightful godly spiritual inheritance. Even though it is difficult to see it in some parents, there is blessing somewhere up the family line that we need to call down to ourselves. Bitterness puts up a wall that shuts off any spiritual family inheritance because we simply can't receive. As a part of this same thing, we all have a masculine and feminine heritage that is passed on to us. Bitterness can shut down and your vow can cut off what God would want passed on to you. The same is true if you have bitterness against the pastor or a teacher in your church.

When an ungodly stronghold rules your life, you find yourself becoming a slave to your thoughts and those thoughts controlling you rather than you controlling your thoughts. When I use this term in this section, I am referring to a negative place that rules, controls, or dominates your thoughts and therefore dictates negative behaviors. When you have a stronghold of bitterness you have lost control of how you feel towards another person or situation. Since bitterness is nothing more than unfulfilled revenge, you stay angry or vengeful in your attitudes even though you might even act cordial on the outside. At this point, you have become enslaved to the bitterness, to the person, or to the situation. They have the power over you. As long as you can't forgive, bondage prevails. Bitterness then becomes the personal damage that you do to yourself because you have chosen to either not forgive or feel powerless to forgive.

It is important to understand that there is a process in which a stronghold is built. Strongholds are not built overnight, but over a period of time when we do not address an issue appropriately by letting grace rule in our hearts. All strongholds begin when we open a door and give the devil a place in which to operate. Ephesians 4:26-27 says, *"In your anger do not sin: Do not let the sun go down while you are still angry, and do not give the devil an* **opportunity.***"*

The word "opportunity" is defined as "opportunity, power, place of operation, an area of legal control." It refers to the first step in opening the door to yielding legal jurisdiction. It is also translated in many different ways. It is translated as "foothold" in the New International Version. The King James Version translates it as "place" while the New Revised Standard says, "Do not make room." The New Century Bible conveys the meaning as it translates the verse—"Do not give the devil a way to defeat you."

The devil wants a base of operation in our lives. Although we have protection by what Christ did on the cross on our behalf, we can still provide such a place if we choose to harbor sin. Once we surrender some real estate in our hearts, the devil seeks to build on it. He doesn't rule the whole heart, only the block we let him move into. From there, a stronghold is methodically constructed until this structure of thoughts dominates our minds and is followed by behaviors.

A stronghold of bitterness starts off when we do not deal immediately with offenses. We open the door when we do not forgive and it becomes the devil's opportunity, his foothold because we gave him room. As long as we allow thoughts of unforgiveness in our heart, we are yielding our thought life to the kingdom of darkness. The demonic thoughts of blame, accusations, self-condemnation, and hate are given the legal right to dwell in our lives. Our demonic adversary wants us to self-destruct with our own bitterness. These thoughts of bitterness are so entrenched in our hearts and mind that we essentially become ruled by them. It is at this point that we can find ourselves helpless to forgive. It is best to be aware of these "opportunities" or "footholds" that open the door and give permission for a stronghold of darkness to become eventually built. Retaining an offense rather than releasing an offense is the first open door.

We can open doors when we entertain a lie and lies become embedded when we believe them. The progression could happen like this: an event occurs in which there is a wounding of the heart. It may have been an actual malicious action that wounded you, or you may have been hurt by your perception of the event as viewed through your filters. Either way, the kingdom of darkness was present to whisper lies into your mind that you received as truth. These lies could be things such as,

"They really don't care about me...They think I am worthless...I am not as loved as my sister (or brother)... They would rather be married to someone else than to me... God hates me...God only created me because He wanted someone to torment...They only want to destroy me...I have to punish them...There is no one else to hold this offense against them, so it is up to me...They don't deserve to be forgiven...Someone has to remember what they did."

These thoughts may or may not have actual merit; however, it doesn't matter because they *feel true to you.*

When you refuse to forgive, because you have a "right" not to forgive, you not only give the devil a place, or a foothold in an area of your soul, but you are now feeding it. The longer you wait to forgive, the harder it is for you to forgive. The deeper a root grows, the more difficult it is to remove. Though nothing is impossible to God, He demands our cooperation for its removal. The deeper it grows, the more unwilling we become to let the Lord run deep in our lives. To make matters worse, what may reinforce those roots could be the inner vows we make that hold us bondage such as *"I will never forgive!"*

Tearing Down the Stronghold of Bitterness
By Rodney Hogue

The following steps are designed to assault the inroads of bitterness and dismantle them.

RECOGNIZE it for what it is: UNFORGIVENESS IS SIN. The first step in ridding yourself of an area of bondage is to agree with how God sees it. Recognition means that you admit it and confess it to God. Confession means to come into agreement with God. You must see it as God sees it: SIN. What happens when you confess? 1 John 1:9 says, "If we confess our sins, He is faithful and righteous to forgive us our sins and to cleanse us from all unrighteousness."

REVOKE the legal right for bitterness to remain: CHOOSE to forgive.

Bitterness remains because of a legal right. You hang onto the offense because you gave ground to it. You allocated a piece of real estate in your heart to the offense and gave it a right to stay. When you open the door, the demonic strives to keep it open. The demonic are legalists. They attempt to enforce what legal right has been turned over to them. If you've opened the door, you have to close it and ask for the keys back. In this step you expose the lie that has kept you in bondage and remove the legal right for the bitterness to stay. You take back the ground you surrendered. You are, essentially serving eviction papers to bitterness.

Now go to the Lord in prayer and take back the ground by praying through the following areas:

- ✞ Seek forgiveness for your part of the offense.
- ✞ Renounce your rights to not forgive.
- ✞ Renounce your inner vows to not forgive.
- ✞ Renounce the lie you have believed.

☦ Make a conscious choice to forgive, even if the feelings of forgiveness are not there.

☦ Release your offender into the hands of Jesus so the he or she will no longer have power over you.

REGAIN: Ask God to regain the surrendered ground that gave a "foothold" or "opportunity" for bitterness to take root.

Realize that God desires to bring restoration to the soul. You must deliberately ask Him to take back the ground given and to remove any bitterness. In this step you will be asking God to remove any right to go back and rekindle your bitterness. This is significant because one the "right" to not forgive has been revoked and that ground is regained, you can no longer justify harboring resentment.

In this step you are reinforcing the eviction notice. You are calling on God to uproot and boot bitterness as an unwanted squatter. You are declaring that that piece of real estate has a new landlord, Jesus, and he's been given full authority over it. Nothing comes in unless it comes in through Jesus.

REMOVE the stronghold of bitterness and REPLACE it with God's truth.

In the next few steps you are going to dismantle old thoughts and replace them with new ones. You are giving Jesus, your new landlord, remolding rights over these regained area. As long as you withhold forgiveness, you are hanging onto your perceived right to punish your offender. It is never your job to punish your offender. That is always God's job. If you retain the sin and refuse to release it, then you are standing in God's way, hindering rather than helping, as God does His job. You must assault that old thought pattern with the truth of God's Word. You must release your offender into the hands of God and declare that you have no right to bring retaliation.

When you take matters into your own hands in order to "get even" with your offenders, you miss out on the special blessing that God gives to those who choose to conquer by love. You also bring destruction to your own physical health, attitudes, and relationships.

REPENT of any false identity you have received from your offenders and REPLACE these with the truth of who you are.

You might not be able to get close to others because you have established emotional walls around yourself. Or, you might gravitate to the other extreme and open yourself to everything and everyone with little regard to healthy boundaries because you want to be accepted and loved. You might have emotional reactions that have developed because of emotional wounding. You might have fears in certain areas that dominate you. The behavioral and emotional reactions can be so ingrained in you that you feel like that is who you are or who you have become, but that isn't true. Your true identity is not found in how you have been shaped by others. It is found in God who made you and in the freedom that you find in Christ. In getting free you may need to identify the areas you have embraced in your perceived identity that aren't the "real" you. These areas must be recognized as a false identity. Our true identity can be found in Christ. Therefore, you must let go by repenting of these false identities and embrace who you are in Christ.

You might really be a caring person but because you've been hurt, you have shut that part of your heart down. You might really be friendly, but offenses have made you guarded and apprehensive about letting people in. Offenses may have caused you to be more cautious and fearful, rather than courageous and bold. The real you may want relationships, while the wounded heart avoids people. You may consider yourself a critical person or judgmental in nature. However, that isn't who you are, but, rather, that is what you have embraced.

For this step you are going to have to list the person, the offense, and then the false identity. The false identity can be: how you see yourself, a reaction you have, a fear you possess, a struggle you have in relating to others, a wall that you set up to protect yourself, an ungodly lifestyle you have, a negative tendency in your character, a sin you gravitate to, or anything else you have taken ownership of because of the offenses of others. As you list the offenders and their offenses, make sure you have released them in forgiveness. Confess to God your part in taking on the false identity. Repent and renounce that false identity and then declare you true identity of who you really are in Christ!

Building a righteous stronghold of compassion will give you power to sustain forgiveness and stay free. Building a godly stronghold requires giving time and attention to not only dismantle unwanted thought patterns, but to renewing the mind to building godly thought patterns. Meditation is necessary to saturate your heart with truth. Meditation is dwelling on a scripture or truth, chewing on it as you would chew on a stick of gum, and letting it sink into your heart. To build a stronghold of compassion, you need to spend time meditating on God's forgiveness for you.

Pastor Rodney continues:

Receive The Grace To Demonstrate Mercy Just As God Has Shown You Mercy And Forgiven You.

God desires to demonstrate mercy to us. Even though we deserve consequences because of our sin against God, mercy means that God chooses to release us from those consequences. You do not show mercy because someone deserves it. You choose to give mercy because you have received God's mercy.

Earlier, grace was defined as the unmerited inexhaustible power supply that flows from God to us and through us to do His will. Grace is closely associated with mercy in that it is available based on God's choice to give it, not on your merit to receive it. Receiving grace means that you have God's power available to you to forgive and show mercy. God's grace is available to all who will receive it. As you have received the grace of God you are empowered to forgive.

Love with the Father's Love

If you know the Lord, you have His love in you. This is the kind of love He imparts to us through His Spirit. You can walk in that love when you walk in the Spirit. When we receive His love for us, we become infused with a love from above that is far beyond what this world offers. We become empowered to love with God's love. It is a love that does not require a love in return. It is a love that overshadows the sins of others and becomes the dominant ruling force in life. Love covers a multitude of sin. His great limitless love can manifest itself through limited humanity.

Love requires you to ask God to help you see your offender through his eyes. This needs to be a conscious choice on your part. It needs to be a prayer request that stays on your petition list. It reminds you daily that eyes of compassion come only from God. Love requires you to erase any record of wrong daily. True love keeps no record of wrong. You do not let those past wrongs suffered rule how you relate to people; instead, you let God's love rule your relationships. To love with God's means realizing that His love is already in us. We just need to exercise it to activate it. Since you know it is God's desire to forgive, you must determine that you will forgive before an offense happens. This is the lifestyle of choice. The only way you could forgive in the way that Jesus did is to determine you will forgive, even before an offense occurs. God wants you to become unoffendable.

We need to also forgive ourselves when we are overwhelmed with guilt and self-condemnation. Self-pity and self-condemnation will cause a person to stay disabled. It is as if you feel like you need to punish yourself a little more than after you have suffered a sufficient amount of pain, then you can reenter the world.

As you spend time with the Lord, let Him bring to mind what He wants you to repent of, not what you feel guilty for. Then confess to God your failure. When you confess, claim the promise of 1 John 1:9, that God will forgive and cleanse you. Next is the difficult part—receive God's forgiveness. This is usually more difficult because of the accusations of the enemy that come storming in and telling you that you are unworthy of such forgiveness. They are thoughts put into your mind by the kingdom of darkness to keep you in defeat. Tell those thoughts to leave in the authority of Jesus. You have been bought with a price, you belong to the kingdom of light, and Jesus, alone, determines your value. This value is determined by what one is willing to pay. Jesus gave His life for you, and that is your value! Your debt has been paid in full. Just as you received Jesus into your heart by faith of salvation, you receive God's forgiveness by faith for cleansing of the heart.

Though some know up front that they are angry and bitter against God, with others it is not that clear. Yet, in their hurt and expectations of Him, they are exactly that—angry at God. He already knows you are angry with Him. He needs you to be honest with your feelings in order for Him to set you free. Anger or resentment against God usually comes because we have an unfulfilled expectation of God. We do not understand how an all-powerful being would allow such suffering and pain. We do not understand how a God who claims to love can allow unloving things to happen. We have these expectations because we project onto God what we feel He should do to fix the situation. We want God to be codependent and to fix everything and do not understand why He does not.

God always looks beyond the present and makes decisions regarding our lives based on how we will spend our eternity. We often do not understand this because we do not see the big picture of His plan for us. We have to understand that he is interested in getting us as prepared as possible for eternity. In our finite minds we can't see that far. We can only see the present. Because His perspective is perfect, there are some things that He causes to happen. There are other things He chooses to allow to happen. Either way, God is still in control. God's plan for our lives includes pain and suffering as He prepares us for a glorious future. Ultimately we will need to come to that place where the lies we believed about God will need to be exposed and confronted so that the power of darkness has no power over you.[137]

You now see how important forgiveness is, as Rodney Hogue has pointed out.

FORGIVENESS OF AN ORPHAN HEART

The first step in the process to healing the Orphan Heart is to forgive those who hurt us, to forgive ourselves, and to forgive God. The decision to forgive is for our benefit and not for the benefit of the person who we choose to forgive. It releases us from the bondage of the pain associated with the unforgiveness. One of the major blocks to any healing experience is *unforgiveness*. Unforgiveness is like acid. It will eat a hole through a can. When

Jesus hung on the cross and said, "Father forgive them, for they know not what they do." He gave us a beautiful example of how we are to treat those who have wounded us. There is always healing after forgiveness. You must be able to say, "Yes I am willing to forgive." You may not feel like forgiving someone. However, forgiveness is not a feeling, it is a decision. You choose to forgive someone. The gift to enable you to forgive comes from God. When you find it difficult to love someone, God's love enables you to love that person. If you can't forgive, Jesus forgiveness enables you to forgive that person. When you pray, pray like this, "Lord help me to forgive all who have wounded me in my past and future experiences. I pray this in your Holy Name Jesus Christ."

However, once the choice is made, forgiveness is not complete until it is forgiveness that comes from the heart. Forgiveness from the heart frees the emotions from the pain. When love is flowing freely again from your heart toward the person who hurt you, that is when forgiveness is complete. They might not receive it but it still is complete.[138]

For if you forgive others for their transgressions, your heavenly Father will also forgive you. But if you do not forgive others, then your Father will not forgive your transgressions. *(Matthew 6:14-15)*

Jesus makes it very clear in scripture that God will forgive us; but if we refuse to forgive others, God will refuse to forgive us.

1. For World War II fatherless children, forgive your father for not being there for you every time you needed your biological father's love and affirmation.
2. For all other orphans, forgive your father for not being emotionally there for you every time you needed your father's love and affirmation.

3. Forgive your parents for misrepresenting Father's love to you.
4. Ask your parents to forgive you for the way you hurt or disappointed them.
5. Lift up to God all the things about God that bothers you.
6. Lift up to God all the things about you that bothers God.

Mark Stibbe relates in his book *From Orphans to Heirs* that he had difficulty to be alone with the Father. His wife determined that it was related to being abandoned by his father when he was a baby. At a Toronto Airport Fellowship "Catch the Fire" conference, a women came to him. She pointed at his heart and said, "Father, minister to the sense of abandonment in this man's heart."[139] Later the speaker John Arnott announced that "many people have a ball and chain around their feet...The golden key is in your hands and this will unlock your chains. Forgiveness is the golden key. So forgive those who have hurt and rejected you"

Mark writes: "As he said those words, I knew exactly what I had to do. I shouted out, 'I forgive you, Dad. I forgive you for abandoning me and rejecting me. I release you right now from my unforgiveness. May the Lord bless you, wherever you are.'"

"As I said this, the peace of God saturated me. I felt totally set free from the fear of rejection. I felt liberated from the slavery that had been oppressing me...As soon as that was complete, intimacy with God was restored."[140]

Confess and renounce your orphan heart. Daily renounce ungodly beliefs and hidden lies of orphan thinking.

7. Ask for forgiveness from those that you have hurt because of your orphan heart.

Unforgiveness is a two way street. In order for us to be free from bondage of unforgiveness, we need to ask for forgiveness from those we have hurt through our life's journey. Only then can healing begin toward receiving the Father's love. I recently had to attend a cousin's funeral in Detroit Michigan. I drove up to Pennsylvania to stay overnight with my daughter and attend Sunday church services with her before driving on to Detroit. We sat in the choir loft and next to her sat my ex-wife with whom I have been friendly for years. Suddenly I felt the Lord place on my heart that I was in bondage by unforgiveness and I needed to ask my ex wife to forgive me. After the services, I asked my ex wife if we could talk and explained to her about the orphan spirit. I explained to her that that is why I treated her so badly and why I was not intimate with her. I asked her to forgive me for abandonment, rejection and the feelings of being unwanted and unloved that I had caused her. I was pouring my heart out to her almost pleading for forgiveness. Her reply was shocking. She said, "Bruce, I forgave you years ago." It was then I knew that asking for forgiveness was not for her or from her, but it was for my benefit. I now knew that I was forgiven and that I could move on with my life towards the Father.

In *Healing Life's Hurts* Dennis and Matthew Linn explain:

Christ uses a twofold forgiveness to bring emotional health (Luke 24:13-35). Though the Emmaus disciples know that Christ's death fills them with anxiety about their future, and with fear that life has lost its meaning. The insight alone doesn't give them the power to change their depression. Rather, power to change comes when they meet the unconditional forgiveness of Christ that helps them work through anger and guilt.

In walking at their pace, Jesus accepts the disciples'
angry feelings toward the chief priests and leaders for
putting the Messiah to death, and toward the prophets
for apparently misleading the disciples. No doubt, too,
Christ knows they feel guilty and downcast about being
foolish men (Luke 24:25). They probably ask themselves,
"Why didn't we listen when Christ warned us he would
die? Why didn't we stand in for him? Why didn't we have
the courage to stay with fearful friends, hiding from the
authorities in Jerusalem?" After Jesus explains the Scriptures to them, they can indeed plead guilty to being foolish, but they need not be depressed about their foolishness,
because it puts them in touch with a forgiving Christ.

**Continued paraphrase from *Healing Life's Hurts* by Den-
nis Linn and Matthew Linn:**

Later at dinner, Jesus gives them the feeling of being
loved unconditionally that creates forgiving hearts that
burn within them. The disciples return to Jerusalem to
extend unconditional love to the people who put Christ
to death, as Christ extended it to them. The memory of
the Messiah's death no longer makes them fearful or anxious. By healing the memory through a twofold forgiveness, Christ brings health as he helps us work through
anxiety, fear, anger, and guilt behind emotional neurosis
and instability.[141]

Focus your life on submitting your mind, body, and soul
to the Father. The root of feeling like a spiritual orphan
is one of the greatest hindrances to people receiving their
healing and walking in expressed love, intimacy, and in
healthy relationships. It takes basic trust being restored
in order to daily feel secure enough to receive the love that
is needed to heal our wounded hearts. The more love and
comfort we are able to receive, the less fearful we are of

opening our hearts to intimate, loving relationships. We must be willing to let go of our need to suppress our childhood pain and to control our emotions in order to open our hearts to receive the Father's healing love and to walk in true intimacy with others.

That is a defining moment, when basic trust was lost, and your ability to receive love and healing was hindered. Find a quiet place to pray and wait upon the Lord. Let your memory get in touch with the emotions of that day. Where was Jesus that day? You were not alone. From the moment you were conceived in your mother's womb, God has not left nor forsaken you (Psalms 22:9-10; 139:13-24; Isaiah 49:15-16; Hebrews 13:5-6). He has promised not to leave you feeling like an orphan. He will come to you (Psalms 27:10; John 14:18-23). There has never been a moment in time when God has not pursued you with His love and sought to purify, cleanse, and restore you (Jeremiah 1:5; 31:3; Isaiah 53:4-5; 66:11-13).[142]

Displacing the Orphan Heart

R everend Martin is a teacher and instructor at Shiloh Place Ministries who teaches on such topics as Healing the Orphan Heart, Experiencing the Father's Embrace, The Father Heart of God, and The Reality of Sonship. In addition he has several DVDs out on the subjects. The following are taken from some of his teachings.

DISPLACING THE ORPHAN HEART
By Reverend Harold Martin

From the very conception of mankind in the heart of the Father God, we were created to be sons and daughters. (For clarification, when we speak of sons, we are not speaking gender specific but instead mean sons and daughters) We were created on purpose, with a purpose, and for a purpose. 1 John 4:16—God is love. We were created by love, for love, and to love. We were created for sonship, created as objects of the Father's affections. We were created to be vessels of his love, to receive his love, and give it away to the world around us.

195

The sad reality is that this is very foreign to most Christians today. Most believers struggle with both giving and receiving love. They struggle with purpose, with having a destiny, and really struggle with sonship.

If the basic concepts of sonship are foundational to our existence, why is there such a struggle for us to be what we were created to be? What happened to the process? What has interrupted the plan of God for his creation?

Ezekiel 28:12 is a description of the fall of Lucifer. He was the anointed guardian cherub until he sinned. Pride is what led to his fall (Isaiah 14:12).

The mindset that drove that choice made Satan the original orphan. He became the role model for all emotional orphans. The motive in the heart of Satan was that he wanted to be like God. Angels were never created to be like God. They were created to be the servants of those who would be the heirs of salvation, i.e., they would become the servants of the sons. The result was that Satan has always been jealous of the position of sons. He has the ultimate goal to destroy, diminish, and devalue sonship. Only sons were created in the image and likeness of God. Sons were created to be like God, not angels.

Look at the creation of sons and daughters: Genesis 1:26—then God said, "Let us make man in our image, in our likeness." The word "image" comes from the Hebrew word "tselem." Image means resemblance. It refers to things that are intangible. Likeness comes from the Hebrew word "demooth." Demooth means "model, shape, fasten, similitude, and bodily resemblance." It refers to things that are tangible. We were created in both the tangible and intangible likeness of God.

Genesis 1:28—God blessed them (he empowered them to prosper) and said to them, "Be fruitful and increase in number; fill the earth and subdue it. Rule over the fish of the sea and the birds of the air and over every living creature that moves on the ground."

Luke 2, from the Amplified version, tells us, no word of God is void of the power necessary to cause it to come to pass. We were created in the image and likeness of God and empowered to do all that he created us to do. The Father revealed this at the tower of Babel in Genesis 11:6. He said, "Nothing they plan to do will be impossible for them." As a child of God, if you can dream it, you can do it.

Genesis 2:7—man was created in the image and likeness of God. He was designed, formed, and fashioned with the capacity to have communion, fellowship, and intimacy with the Father. The lord God formed the man from the dust of the ground and breathed into his nostrils the breath of life, and the man became a living being. Think about it. How close did God have to get to Adam to breathe the breath of life into his nostrils? Have you ever wondered how he did it? Was it a short puff or did he blow a gust of air like performing CPR?

What did Adam see when he opened his eyes? The face of God, which was the face of his Father. He was looking into the eyes of perfect love, agape love. When God breathed the breath of life into the nostrils of Adam, He imparted himself, his seed, the DNA of God into his son. 1 John 3:8 tells us that seed, that deposit of the person of our Father remains in us.

The Father gave him a wife because it was not good for the man to be alone. We were created for relationships, safe productive loving relationships. He blessed them. The blessing was the empowerment to prosper and was the empowerment to accomplish the mission the Father had given them: be fruitful, multiply, fill the earth, and subdue it. The Father's mission was to make the rest of the world just like the garden. The heart of Father God is for all creation to live in Eden, a home of abundance, a home of intimacy, and a place where love and acceptance freely flows.

God's seed that remains in us, the DNA that God deposited in us at creation, continually cries out to be reconnected with the Father. The deposit deep within you is crying out to the deep things of God. The deep things of God are not the news, weather, and sports of the universe. It is not why the world turns or even what is about to happen in our world. The deep crying out to deep is the cry for intimacy. In the garden, the Father came down in the cool of the day and walked with Adam and Eve. They shared an intimate relationship with the Father. Intimacy with you was his plan from the very beginning of time. The cry from deep within us is to once again be embraced by our Father. Our hearts continually longs to experience the Father's embrace. He wants to place you in the position where you can continually experience His embrace. The cry is to return to our "as created" position of sonship. We were designed, created, formed, and fashioned to be sons and daughters. We were created to live in sonship. All that he has done throughout the ages, all that he accomplished and provided by the blood of Jesus, was done to return you to that "as created" position of sonship. This is the cry of our hearts. It is our purpose. It is our destiny.

Genesis 2:8—now the lord God had planted a garden in the east, in Eden; and there he put the man he had formed. God had planted a garden. The Father had prepared the place for his son before the son was created. The atmosphere and experience of the garden was God's original plan for man. He has not changed his mind. Eden was for pleasure, delight; was voluptuous; and had abundant supply. The abundant supply of the garden was not just natural physical stuff, but was also an abundance of the presence of the Father. It was the perfect home for the perfect son.

Genesis 3—the goal of the temptation of Adam and Eve was to remove man out of the mindset of sonship and put him into orphan mentality. The temptation was to destroy the vision man had of Father. To destroy man's ability to see Father as the abundant provider and begin to see him as distant, non relational, and the one who was holding out on man. Not allowing man to be all he had the potential to be. The temptation was to seek knowledge, self reliance, and independence rather than trust and intimacy. Up to that point, Adam and Eve had a relationship with the Father that was based on trust, dependency, and love. Deception can be very deceiving. Satan tempted Eve through doubt and deception clothed in shame to entice Eve into disobedience. Adam who was right there with her followed her down the path of disobedience. They chose to replace faith and trust with knowledge.

Trust is the foundation of faith. It is the fruit of a relationship in which you know you are loved. Up to this point Adam and Eve lived in that place with the Father. Over and over again the Bible tells us to watch out that we are not deceived. When you begin to play with fire, you are taking the first step to being burned. When you begin to entertain thoughts that are contrary to the word or will of God, you are taking the first steps towards sin and orphan mentality. Through the fall by the deception of Satan, whereby Adam and Eve chose to disobey the Father, sin separated Father and son. Trust was now replaced with fear. We have recently learned that when trust is lost or diminishes, fear will always come to replace it. Now instead of walking in the cool of the day with God, they were hiding from God because they were afraid.

We all need to understand that there is no such thing as private sin. The sin of Adam and Eve did not affect just them. Their sin became generational. Their sin imparted a sin nature or the natural tendency towards sin into all following generations. We are the seed from their seed. Their sin ultimately required the blood of the Son of God to bring about justification and forgiveness. Sin separated the Father from his son. It caused a breach in fellowship and loss of intimacy. Through sin and disobedience, not only did man receive the impartation of a sin nature from Satan's deception but he also received the impartation of Satan's orphan heart/orphan mentality. From that point forward, orphan mentality became a generational issue. We are all born with a tendency to move into orphan mentality rather than live in sonship. Now instead of all creation being in tune with man, the creation waits in eager expectation for the sons of God to be revealed.

THE ORPHAN HEART
By Rev. Harold Martin

What is it and is its conditions

Orphan mentality/an orphan heart are not spirits that can be cast out. Orphan mentality is an acquired way of thinking. It is a heart attitude. The orphan heart/ orphan mentality is one of self reliance which believes one must do it myself. One of independence which believes one cannot trust or depend on anyone else for anything. Orphan mentality would rather shop at the tree of knowledge than the tree of life. It thinks it can be like God through its own efforts. An orphan heart feels like it has no place to call home. It has no place of total acceptance, belonging, warmth, comfort, protection, security, and identity. It has no a place where you are given a sense of purpose and destiny. It has no place where you receive affirmation and encouragement. And most of all it has no place where, no matter what mistakes you may make, you know you have a safe place in the Father's heart. A place that you can run to. A place where you are loved unconditionally.[143]

A person suffering from an orphan heart feels like they have no one to love them. They believe they do not have a safe place in the Father's heart. God cannot be trusted and cannot be depended on. They feel like they must do it all themselves, be independent, and be a self made person. (Why did you make such a mess?) Their life is filled with all types of fears. They struggle with relationships. James Jordan states that loneliness is not being alone or by yourself. Loneliness is not having anyone to share your heart with. For most people with orphan mentality the basic emotional needs of life are not being met. Remember the basic emotional needs are: security, love, affirmation, and purpose.

Remember also that this is beyond the reality of whether or not these needs are being supplied but the feeling that they are being supplied. Not having these needs met creates pain in your heart and pain always seeks pleasure. We look for something to numb the pain even if is it only temporary. The result when the basic needs of life go unmet is that we end up chasing after the counterfeit affections. We look for love and the right answers in all the wrong places.

A person with orphan mentality will struggle with all their relationships. They are driven by a need to be needed. All of their relationships look like two ticks and no dog. They go around with their IV needle in hand looking for someone to plug into. **They are just looking for someone to make them feel safe, loved, and affirmed. Someone to make them feel like there is some real reason for them to be here.** As previously stated, an orphan heart is a generational issue. Father's beget sons, but orphans beget orphans. The attitude of society today amplifies orphan mentality. The world thinks this is normal. We teach it in our schools. We preach it in our churches. Orphan mentality is everywhere you look today. The result is our relationships are a mess and are all shattered and scattered. The divorce rate in the church is greater than 50 percent.

Why is orphan mentality so prevalent in the world today? An orphan heart is perpetuated through wounding. Wounding perpetuates orphan thinking. We all have negative life experiences. An orphan heart is the result of our wrong responses to life's negative experiences. When we are wounded or have a negative life experience, Satan plants a lie in our hearts that establishes a negative belief. Whatever you believe to be true is true to you even if it is a lie. That belief will produce a negative expectancy that will cause a negative behavior. Our wrong response is the result of a lie we believed when the negative experience happened. Our wrong response will cause a negative experience which perpetuates the cycle. The only way to break the cycle is to change what you believe foundationally about you. You are not an orphan. You are a son/daughter.

Any time you are wounded or someone fails to properly demonstrate the Father's love to you, the Father of lies will tell you a lie about yourself, God, or others. When you believe that lie and accept it as the truth you begin to live out the negative consequence of the lie every day. For you, the lie may as well be true because the consequence in your life will be the same as if it were true. These lies create strongholds in your mind or fortresses of thought. These strongholds develop into habit structures of thinking that will exalt themselves above the truth of the word of God. The stronghold of orphan thinking exalts itself above your knowledge of the word of God. Orphan thinking, orphan mentality, and having an orphan heart are the greatest strongholds Christians deal with. No matter how many times someone tells you the truth or you read it in your Bible, you still believe the lie.

Sonship

My father was an alcoholic. He was never there when I needed him. He never came to my baseball games, he was not around for holidays, birthdays or graduations. Once, while playing ball I ended up in the hospital for two days. He didn't know where I was. He had dropped me off at the game and went drinking. Later in life I discovered the reason for my father's drinking and rejection of me. My father never believed I was his son. He emotionally divorced himself from me before I was born. Therefore, I developed orphan mentality before I came into the world. My attitude was if it is going to happen I have to do it. I became so self reliant, so much of an orphan in thought and attitude, that for much of our married life I caused my wife to feel like I didn't need her. I could get along fine staying busy in my own little world. My orphan mentality strained our relationship until I heard the revelation of the Father's love and began my journey into sonship. I am still on that journey and enjoying the trip.

You are the person you are because of the father you have. You are born a child, however you mature into being a son. Many never make it into sonship. Remember when the Jews claimed to be descendants of Abraham. Jesus quickly told them natural linage does not make you a son. Your action, your attitude, and your behavior declare whose son you are. Like Father, like son.

Being at home in the Father and walking in our position of sonship is indicated by how comfortable you are with love. Both giving and receiving love. It is how comfortable you are with the concept of crawling up in the Father's lap and how comfortable are you with manifestations of the Father's presence. Are you more prone to judge and evaluate than you are to participate and enjoy? How much we feel at home with the Father and how much we feel he is at home with us indicates how we are doing at walking in the spirit of sonship the Father has given us. Remember we were created for sonship and intimacy with the Father.

Romans 8:19—the creation waits in eager expectation for the sons of God to be revealed. All creation is waiting in eager anticipation and expectancy for us, the sons and daughters of the Father God, to step into the position we were created to occupy. The position of sonship.

Jesus came to restore us to sonship. The entire plan of salvation is all about the restoration of man back to his "as created" position of sonship. The restoration of intimacy, trust and even our salvation, is all about displacing the orphan heart and replacing the heart of sonship. Sons have an inheritance. To receive our inheritance as mature sons we must listen to the voice of the Father. We must be submitted to his mission for our life which is our destiny. If we are not submitted to the Father and his mission for our life, we open ourselves up to become subject to orphan mentality. The Father's mission and his will for your life is sonship. Sonship includes living in intimacy with the Father and enjoying the blessings of heaven right here on earth.

There is a test for sonship. John 14:21—whoever has my commands and obeys them, he is the one who loves me. He who loves me will be loved by my Father, and I too will love him and show myself to him. In our position as children of God we are totally loved and accepted in Christ. But there is difference between being a child and being a son. Sonship usually comes though obedience and patience that is learned through suffering. Suffering is not sickness, disease, disaster, or tragedy. Suffering is what your soul and flesh go through when being conformed to your born again spirit. The flesh suffers when it does not get its way nor gets to act the way it wants to.

Just because Father can do some amazingly wonderful things with incredibly bad situations does not mean he authored the situation. God does not cause, create, or allow evil just so he can do good. If he did he would be working against what Jesus did. His house would be divided. The lack of understanding and the lack of revelation of the Father's love will cause us to blame God for what the devil does and for what we do to ourselves. This lack of understanding keeps us out of sonship and living in bondage to orphan mentality.

Heb 5:7-8—during the days of Jesus' life on earth, he offered up prayers and petitions with loud cries and tears to the one who could save him from death, and he was heard because of his reverent submission. Although he was a son, he learned obedience from what he suffered and, once made perfect, he became the source of eternal salvation for all who obey him.

Sonship is learned. You mature into sonship through obedience and suffering, i.e., bringing your flesh and soul into submission to your spirit. Jesus was our example.

In Luke 2, we see the story of Jesus at 12 years old teaching the Pharisees in the temple in Jerusalem. They were amazed at the depth of revelation Jesus had. After three days his parents discover he is not traveling with them. His parents come looking for him. Luke 2:46—they found him in the temple courts, sitting among the teachers, listening to them and asking them questions. Jesus said to his parents, "Didn't you know that I had to be in my Father's house?" Some translations say, "about my Father's business." His parents take Jesus home with them. He continued in subjection to his earthly parents. He knew he had to have sonship with earthly parents first in order to enter into his inheritance with his heavenly Father.

When we reject a spirit of sonship with our parents because they "lack revelation" we reject it with God. Jesus stayed obedient to His earthly parents and so grew in wisdom, stature, and favor with God and man.

Remember how uncool your parents were. How they embarrassed you by being so old-fashion and not knowing everything like we did. I was amazed how much my parents learned from the time I was 13 until I was 21.

In the culture of Jesus' time, 12 years old was the time of going from childhood into apprenticeship. At 30 you would receive your inheritance and your Father would set you up in business. At 30 we see Jesus receiving his inheritance as a good son. History indicates he had finished his rabbinical training. He came to John the Baptist to be baptized and received the affirmation of his Father. This is my beloved son in whom I am well pleased.

The affirmation of the Father not only released Jesus into his ministry and into his inheritance but it also carried him from His baptism to the cross. His ministry was revealing the Father and proclaiming the kingdom of heaven is at hand. His inheritance was you. His inheritance was the multitudes of sons and daughters coming into the kingdom. A Moravian mission motto says: May the Lamb of God receive the reward of his suffering. Jesus suffered to pave the way for your sonship. His blood was poured out for your forgiveness. His body was scourged for your healing; the humiliation/brokenness, defeat of death, hell, and the grave set you free from demonic torment and gave you authority over all the power of the enemy. He suffered to enable us to live in sonship, to live in the kingdom of heaven right here on earth, and to live in intimacy with the Father.

The voice of the Father empowers the son. The voice of the Father provides security for the son. Jesus Christ is perfect theology. He is the prototype for all sons and daughters to follow. We see that He first submitted to and honored his earthly parents. He was also submitted to the spiritual authorities set over him. He received the affirmation of his Father and was empowered to overcome temptation by the enemy. There is no mountain too high, no challenge too difficult, and no devil too big, when you know the Father is right there with you.

In the wilderness the devil came against Jesus with orphan thinking; take care of yourself, do things your own way, follow me, become subject to my mission for your life rather than God's. Rejecting orphan thinking and being consumed by the spirit of God, equipped, and empowered Jesus to fulfill his ministry. Being a son is what will equip you for life and will equip you to be a Father. The bottom line is; with every challenge of life you have a choice. Hear the voice of the Father and deal with it as a son or hear the voice of the devil and be defeated by it as an orphan.

Satan is out to destroy sonship. He was the original orphan and misery loves company. How is this orphan heart/orphan mentality playing out in the world today? Just think about the number of natural orphans that are in the world. In America most of the babies born last year were born to single moms. A staggering 50% of the children in America will go home each night without a Father. Add to that the thousands of fathers and mothers that are killed in the wars we have been fighting for most of this century, along with those killed by natural disasters, accidents, sickness, and all the tragedies that take a parent out of the home. How hard is it for a person to develop the heart of a son if they are living as an orphan? Remember that Satan's tactic is to destroy sonship.

What is the mindset of most churches today? It is that you must change, stop whatever you are doing, and change to be like us. You must believe exactly like we do. We have all types of membership classes to ensure people believe just like we do. Then, maybe, we will allow you to belong to our club called the church. This mindset is driven by orphan mentality amongst those that are supposed to be leading people into a revelation of the kingdom of God.

How would that change if we all had the heart of a son rather than an orphan? The basic mind set of the church would be that you belong because you are a creation of your Father God. You can come just as you are. We will love you. We will honor you. We will accept you. Once you know you belong and that there really are no hidden agendas, you will begin to believe what the word of God says about you, about God, and about others. When you begin to believe the word of God in an environment of safety and security, and an environment of belonging, change will happen automatically. The change will be from the orphan mentality of the world to the mentality of a son. One dearly loved by the Father. Phenomenal things happen when people begin to understand how much they are loved by the Father.

HEALING YOUR ORPHAN HEART
By Rev. Harold Martin

Orphan mentality and orphan heart are not spirits that can be cast out. Orphan mentality is an acquired way of thinking. It is a heart attitude. It cannot be cast out. It is a stronghold of believing that must be displaced. It is displaced by your personal revelation of the Father's intense love for you and your determination to live in the position of sonship the Father provided for you by the blood of Jesus. It is living in sonship by being submitted to the Father God. Being submitted to the natural and spiritual fathers he has placed in your life is what prepares you and equips you for life as a son.

How do you do that? How can you displace your orphan heart? Go back to Moses and the burning bush. What caught Moses' attention? The bush burned but was not consumed. Moses turned aside to see this strange sight. The bush facilitated the encounter. It was the supernatural presence of God within the bush that captured Moses' attention. The bush was just being a bush. It was the presence of God within the bush that made the difference. It will be the presence of God within you that will make a difference in your world every day. People will turn aside, stop, and take notice when they can see a difference in you. It takes a son to lead you to the Father. An orphan may be able to lead you to the master's house, but only a son can show the way to where you really need to go. Only a son can show you the way home.

An orphan needs a home. Someone that has an orphan mentality needs a homecoming. How do we get to have a homecoming? Luke 15 is a classic example of how a young man who grew up in the home of perfect love was pulled to the pig pen by orphan thinking. This young man valued his inheritance more than the relationship with his father. The prodigal son basically told his father that he wished his father was dead, to give him his inheritance now, and let him get on with his life. That is total orphan thinking. The younger son took the money and went off into the world. He was the life of the party until the money ran out. He ended up broke, alone, and feeding pigs in a foreign land. When he came to his senses, he recognized that the lie he had believed was not the truth. All that was needed for a homecoming was his decision to head on home. Home represents: a place of acceptance, belonging, warmth, comfort, protection, security, identity, a place where you are given a sense of purpose and destiny, a place where you receive affirmation and encouragement. He was an orphan, he received his homecoming, and now he is going to live as a son.

How many of you today need a homecoming? How many of you need to step out of orphan mentality and displace your orphan heart with the heart of sonship. The Father God is waiting to welcome you home. Come to your senses and step out of orphan mentality. Get rid of an orphan heart and step into the reality of sonship. Romans 8:15—for you did not receive a spirit that makes you a slave again to fear, but you received the spirit of sonship. And by him we cry, "Abba, Father."

If you do not feel at home in the Father and do not feel like you have a safe place in the Father's heart, you will struggle with orphan mentality and be in bondage to fear. All types of fear. With orphan mentality, you become subject to the Father of lies. Subject to the deception of the devil.

Genesis 3—Lucifer, Satan himself, deceived Adam and Eve into sin through disobedience to the word and will of the Father. It is the story of how man lost his home and forfeited the place of perfect intimacy with the Father. The story of how man took on the heart of an orphan. Since that time, since the fall of man, the Father has worked to return man to his home, to the place of sonship he was created to live in. All that the Father God accomplished and provided by the blood of Jesus was done to return you to that "as created" position of sonship, your "as created" position of intimacy, to place you in the position where you could continually experience the Father embrace. The Father created a home in him for you and he is determined that Satan will not rob you of that place.

We either live our life as if we have a home in the Father seeking to accomplish his destiny for our life or we live our life as an orphan driven by the demands and dictates of our flesh and jerked around by the devil.

Our daughter is adopted. She is the offspring of her biological father but she is not his daughter, she is mine. We adopted her, we raised her, she is as much ours as our natural born son. She knows this, she understands this, and walks in her position as my daughter. She has all rights and authority to the family name. She has all the privileges of being in our family. She is always protected, always provided for, and always loved. She knows she has a safe place on father's lap.

But what if she chose not to walk in her position? What if she chose to rebel against being our daughter? What if she chose to walk in orphan mentality, not come under our authority, and receive our fathering and mothering? She would forfeit all the blessings associated with our family. Just like the younger son and the older brother in the story of the prodigal. You can live in the Father's house and still not occupy your position as a son or daughter.

How many of you are following Jesus? Do you know where he is taking you? Jesus wasn't the man he was because he was God, he was the man he was because of the Father he had. You do not become like Jesus by focusing your life upon him. You become like Jesus by focusing your life upon what Jesus focused his life upon—the Father God. But those with an orphan heart do not have the faith or expectation for a father to be there when they are in need. They have more faith in what they can do.

It is very difficult to overcome temptation without an experiential revelation of how much the Father loves you. John 8:32—you will know the truth and the truth shall set you free. The word "know" here means "experientially" and "intimately." You cannot replace experiential data with logical information. You need another experience. You need an experience with truth and love. You need the embrace of a Father. We either live life as if we have a home or do not have a home in the Father's heart. It is about how we feel in the Father's presence. We either live our life hearing the voice of our Father saying, "You are my beloved child in whom I am well pleased!" or we hear the voice of the Father of lies saying, "Nobody cares about you, they don't like you, you have no one that loves you!" We either live life like a beloved child who lives to receive God's love and to give it away to the next person we meet or we live life like a slave or servant who constantly strives to earn the right to be in the master's presence.

We were created in the image and likeness of God as sons and daughters. The Father is calling us to daily make the choice in our decisions to walk in sonship. The enemy is also tempting us and luring us into being orphans. The choice is yours. The question is whose son/daughter are you?

Displacing the orphan heart begins with revelation. Both the revelation of the Father's intense love for you and the revelation of how far out of sonship you are currently living. You can go anywhere in the world you want to go from where you are. The key is first of all knowing where you are. Simply examine the fruit of your life. Are you bearing more fruit of an orphan heart or the fruit of sonship.

Once you recognize where you are, begin the process of moving deeper and deeper into sonship. Begin the determined process of renewing your mind to the truth of what God's word says about you and about your position as a dearly loved son. This may require receiving personal ministry to help you remove the lie based thinking that has held you out of the position God created you to live in. Come home—the Father Himself is waiting to welcome you and restore you to your place as a son.

One of the greatest benefits of sonship is receiving the blessing of a father. Throughout the scriptures we see the blessing of the father being greatly sought after. Jacob, with the help of his mother, deceived Isaac into blessing him over the first born Esau. Once the blessing is released, it cannot be taken back, even if it is spoken over the wrong person. The blessing is purposed to declare destiny into the heart of a son. Too many of the sons and daughters in the kingdom of God have never received the blessing of a father. We want to change that for you.[144]

The following is "A Father's Blessing" for you.

A Father's blessing
The events of childhood can shape our future in many ways, by the environment we live in and by the words spoken over us by those who cared for us. If in your childhood you did not receive the blessing of your Father, I, as a Father, want to pronounce a Father's blessing over you, on behalf of the father you may or may not have known. Read these words aloud, receive them into the depths of your of your heart. Receive them as spoken from the heart of your Father. If he had known the importance of a Father's love for his child, he would have declared something similar over you.

First, I cancel every negative word spoken over you. I come against the negative effects of an orphan spirit in your life in Jesus name. I call those effects to nothing. I cancel the effects of any trauma that occurred in your life, from the time you were in the womb till now.

My child, I am sorry for not accepting you just the way God made you. I am sorry for not spending more time with you and taking you places with me. I am sorry for not listening more attentively. I am sorry for not being as tender and loving as I could have. I am sorry I did not tell you often how much I loved you. I am glad that you are my child. I am proud to be your Father. Please know that you are loved, you are wanted, and you are affirmed and appreciated.

Father, I ask that you remove the hurts and pain and heal the wounds my actions have caused in the heart of my child.

A FATHER'S BLESSING

I bless you with:

† The ability to receive and walk in the fullness of God's abundant provision of grace and his gift of righteousness.

† Peace and joy—peace the surpasses understanding—joy that will keep you regardless of your surroundings or circumstances.

† The heart of a good son. A heart that passionately pursues the presence of the Father God.

† Prosperity and success in all you do that all you put your hands to will be blessed.

† Friends that Genuinely care about your well being—friends that will be a blessing to you and you to them.

† Integrity in all you do. A heart that shows honor to others—humility—courage and perseverance.

† Wisdom—insight—revelation and understanding in both spiritual and natural things.

† A life that is long—healthy and happy a tender spirit and a compassionate heart.

† Self worth that you may walk in the fullness of what God created you to be. Self confidence to counter act the negatives of life.

† Knowledge that you may teach others passion that you might share with others the reality of the Father's love.

† A spirit of purity that you might demonstrate holiness to others.

† Basic trust that you might accept others right where they are.

† A sense of belonging that you may never be lonely.

† May you always be quick to forgive—slow to anger—patient and understanding of the faults and failures of others.

† May you be constantly aware of God's presence where Ever you may go.

† May your life always be fully pleasing to God—a blessing to others and fully satisfying to you.

Now I call forth the destiny God has placed in you—I release the fullness of the purposes of God for your life. In Jesus' name. Amen.[145]

PRAYERS FOR HEALING
Shiloh Place Ministry

Love and Intimacy

Inner healing is a process that is like peeling an onion one layer at a time. The journey through this process is sometimes made easier by opening up our hearts through prayer

God has crafted us to be an instrument of His love and to demonstrate His compassion and tenderness to everyone we meet. When we begin to experience His phileo love for us and allow it to flow through us to others, we will begin to be secure in love and intimacy because we will be doing what we were created to do.

It can be helpful to begin opening our hearts to Father's love by praying this kind of prayer:

Father, I come to You in Jesus' name. I believe that I have been created for love, to experience your healing love and to share that love in my relationships with others. It's not enough to have success in my life or in my ministry if I don't have a relationship built upon expressed love with You or with my spouse and family. I renounce the lie that I am not a lover, that I cannot open up my emotions or allow myself to be hurt again. Instead, I ask You to wrap Your arms around me, to comfort me in those areas of hurt and pain and to fill me up so that I can in turn share Your love with those around me. I choose to love my family as Christ loved the church and gave Himself for her. I make a commitment to ask myself hourly, "Father, how can I receive Your love and then give it away to the next person I meet?" I want to live my life as an expression of Your love, no longer focusing on my own worldly successes but allowing Your character to shine through me others. I choose to submit to Your love.

Restoration to Father's Love

Heavenly Father, I come to You in Jesus' name. Thank You for Your love that surpasses my understanding. I long to return to Your house. I confess my sin. Please forgive me for valuing my inheritance and the things I hope to gain for myself more than I value an intimate relationship with You and with others. I have taken my inheritance and consumed it on my own lusts. I took from You what You were so willing to give to me, and I have not been faithful with it. I drifted away from Your house to pursue my own selfish interests, but now I long to return to You. I make a choice to leave the pigpen of sin and shame and to come home. Let me experience Your compassion. Run to me and welcome me back as Your child in Your loving embrace. Restore me to Your love.

Our Homecoming

Heavenly Father, I come before You with a repentant heart. I realize that I have been like an older brother in Your house, often placing the love of the law above the law of love in my heart. I recognize that I have had to deal with attitudes of resentment, competition, striving and jealousy, and I see the damage this has caused to my relationship with you and my relationship with the people I love. I realize how much I require others to perform for my acceptance and love. I have sinned against love.

Father, I choose to turn from these attitudes and return to Your heart of love and compassion, but I am going to need Your help. Restore to me the joy of my salvation, when I was motivated by my love for You and my gratitude for Your sacrifice. I want to serve You with a pure heart, motivated by Your compassion and love for others. Thank You for welcoming me back into Your house and allowing me to join in the celebration. In Jesus' name.

Prayer for Healing from Father Issues

Shiloh Place Ministries School suggests the following prayers to go along with the recommended actions:

Father God, I come to you in Jesus' name. Thank you that the door to Your house is always open to me and I do not have to fear Your loving presence. You tell me in Psalm 45:10 to let go of my identity connected to my Father's house so that I can enter into Your love. I come to You as a child in need of Your help so that I can release and forgive my father.

✝ Choose to forgive your father for each way he hurt and disappointed you. Be detailed in speaking specific words of forgiveness for each moment of wounding that comes to mind. It is very helpful to have someone experienced in healing prayer to pray through these areas with you.

✝ Ask God to show you any specific memory that still influences your thought life, attitudes, or actions. Ask God to enter into that situation and bring comfort to the hurting child. Be still and quietly wait on God's love to touch that area. Let the verses about God's love and comfort come to mind in order to displace distracting thoughts.

✝ Lay your father at the foot of the Cross and release him. Lay at the Cross the pain, the anger, the bitterness, and the disappointments. No turn and walk away.

✝ Renounce the striving and fear from your earthly father's house.

✝ Turn to Father God. "I have nowhere to go for love. I know the door to Your house is always open. You said that You would not leave me like an orphan. I ask You, Father, to come to me now and reveal Your love and Fatherhood for me. I choose to receive You as a Father to me. I choose to be Your child."

✟ Begin to pray, or have someone pray over you, the scriptures about Father's love for you. Meditate upon them throughout the day.

✟ Put on music about Father's love for you and let the message penetrate your heart as you sit quietly meditating upon the Father's love for you. Meditate upon them throughout the day.

✟ Begin reading books on the Father's love.

Prayer for Slumbering Spirits

Thank You, Father God, that at my conception You breathed Your Spirit into me. You created me to be one with You, and to have fellowship with You, spirit to Spirit. Lord, come and minister to my spirit. By your grace and healing power bring me to life. Complete the task that my earthly father failed to do. I forgive my father for not giving me the affection I needed, for not being there for me, for not affirming me, or holding me enough, and for not following God's commandment to fathers; to nurture and awaken my spirit and bring me to life.

Lord, come and awaken my slumbering spirit. Resurrect it unto life. Loose it from the grasp of the enemy. Help me to accept your love and to feel your touch. I bind my spirit to Your Holy Spirit and to Your love. Restore to me fourfold, that which was taken from me in childhood and in life. Restore to me my innocence, zest for life, sensitivity, ability to be intimate with You and others, to have hope, to use my creative abilities, to have spiritual inspiration when I'm in Your presence or when reading Your Word; also to have an awareness of my spirit and the spirits of others, to exhibit vitality and strength of mind, and to have the ability and the desire to experience the glory of sexual union with my spouse.

Lord, I confess to You and repent from my sins of resentment, anger and my bitterness toward my dad, for his failure and omissions. I ask You to loose me from the effects of those sins. Father God, forgive me for the many ways I have withdrawn from intimacy in my life.

Also, for the bitter root judgments and negative expectations I've held in my heart about my dad and others. I acknowledge this as sin and I truly repent. Lord also forgive me for striving to win love and acceptance without the willingness or spiritual ability to hold my heart open to others. In the name of Jesus Christ, I tear down and destroy all the strongholds (habits, attitudes, values, and beliefs) I have built to support my bitterness. Father, I take them all to the Cross of Jesus and I crucify them now and forever. Lord, I ask you to restore all that has been destroyed by my bitter-root judgments against my dad and the other men in my life. Lord, I also ask you to forgive my father and to set him free.

Lord, I am willing (or, help me to be willing) to fully forgive my dad and other men and loose them from my bitter root judgments. I accept Your forgiveness for my sins and I ask you to help me to fully accept your forgiveness and love.

Lord, at this time I declare to You and myself that I choose life, and I choose it more abundantly as your Word promises. I understand that abundant life is one filled with Your peace, love, joy and prosperity. A life where my value is defined by who I am in Jesus Christ and my hope is based on Your grace and love which is never ending. Lord, fill me with life and give me the strength of spirit to persist in risking to choose life. Enable and encourage me to be vulnerable to those whom You send to nurture me (body, mind, spirit and soul). Set me free from this slumber and empower me to bring life and joy to others as You intended.

In Jesus's name,
Amen.[146]

Our Inheritance

Impartation for healing of the orphan spirit from Leif Hetland:

Open your heart now to receive the love of Father God into your heart. Some of you may experience rejection being broken from your life. Let his love flow into those wounded areas of your emotions and remove the hurt and pain of those experiences. Maybe you were abandoned as a child. Maybe you were physically abused by alcoholic parents as a child. Maybe you are the 15-year-old girl that was hiding in the closet. Maybe you had a father that was physically there in your life but not emotionally in your life. Maybe you never were able to experience true intimacy in your relationships. Maybe you have always felt that you are not lovable and no one really cares or likes you. Maybe you have always felt that you were a failure. It is time for you to be healed of your orphan heart.[147]

Conclusion

En arche en ho logos, kai ho logos en pros ton theon, kai theos en ho logos, "In the beginning was the word and the word was with God and the word was God" *(John 1:1).*

Then he created man in His own image.

Then he banished them from the garden and they became orphans. The orphan heart mentality was created. We are a fruit of their seed.

He sent prophets to show His children the Love He had in His Father's heart. However, it took sending His only begotten son to show His love for His children.

At some point in history, children were being separated from their mothers and fathers. Children were being deprived of the nurturing love they were meant to receive. The image of the Father was not being reflected in the love of the earthly father.

Wars came and shame entered into the culture. Illegitimate children were born and soldiers were killed. Purification of countries' gene pools became common and justified.

World War II caused a paradigm shift in the spiritual and emotional culture of the world. **There was a shift back to orphan thinking.** 13 million war children were deprived of their biological parents. They did not experience the Father's love reflected to them through their parents. Some developed orphan hearts. Hidden core pain produced a void in their souls because of a lack of their biological fathers love. Some experienced storge love depravation from their mothers due to an inability to nurture because of the postwar social, emotional, political, and financial conditions. The sins of the fathers are passed down to the third or fourth generation. We now are experiencing the results.

We are in a major pandemic of fatherlessness. According to Pastor Harold Martin, "This is why it is so important for the people in the church to recognize what the devil is doing in your life today. To recognize how far out of your position of sonship you are living. To recognize how deep orphan mentality has become ingrained in your life. To realize how much you are living out of an orphan heart rather than the heart of a son/daughter.

One of the greatest obstacles and biggest strongholds that we need to overcome to be able to move into the reality of our sonship is the pandemic of orphan mentality that has consumed the church and our society of believers. We were created in the image and likeness of God for communion, fellowship, and intimacy with him. Because of all the Father has accomplished by the blood of Jesus, the devil, and all the hordes of hell *cannot* stop us from moving into our "as created" positions of sons and daughters. So, just like in the garden, he uses the deception of orphan thinking, the subtle impartation of the orphan heart to rob us of what belongs to us. The heart of sonship belongs to you. An orphan heart is something that attaches itself to you. We need to recognize the reality of both and understand why we are where we are. We need to begin to move progressively and purposely towards our position of sonship.

It is imperative that we put a stop of orphan heart mentality now so that the Father's love will dam up any further progress down the river that feeds the genetic pool of future generations. The cycle of fatherlessness must be broken.

Bruce Brodowski

Afterword

We began with the premise that World War II was also a spiritual war and that its end effected a paradigm shift in the emotional and spiritual culture of the world. Millions of orphans had no homes and many whose parents were still alive had no idea where they were. Illegitimate children did not know who their fathers were, and many were evacuated from their countries without their mothers, without citizenship, without a home, and in shame. In Europe, children roamed the streets and countrysides in "wolf packs." They begged or stole the food they ate, the sticks to make a fire, old rags for clothes. They sought shelter in the ruins of bombed out buildings in cellars and basements. These would become some of the parents that would shape the future generation.

By the end of 1945, the food shortage became alarming. Food stocks had run out in many towns during the fall, and shattered communications made the labor of replacing them slow. Babies were abandoned by mothers who could not feed them. Children stole scraps of food from Allied depots and scavenged in refuse bins. They also learned to steal coal from the railroad tracks and wood from nearby forests.[148] Some American children grew up fatherless because their daddy's didn't come home. Because of the "wall of silence," many children in many countries knew nothing about their dads. Some orphans have experienced an orphan heart attitude that encompasses a deep dark empty hole in their lives. This was due to the void of a father's influence and love in the home. The lack of a father's affirmation during childhood development created generations of unaffirmed children. For them, this was the consequence of war. We saw that even if a father is physically present in the home, a child could still feel fatherless.

We presented the history of the orphan heart, where it began, and some examples of it in scripture. We defined what an orphan heart attitude was like and the importance of relationship and intimacy. We presented the similarities and differences between the orphan heart, orphan spirit, and spiritual orphan attitude. We looked at our image of God and how we see God. We saw through the doctrine of adoption and sonship that God wants a close intimate fellowship with each of us.

So where do we go from here? Healing is a journey with the Father that has a beginning but continues for a lifetime. Progress in this journey is a process in the Father's love. As long as you have progress, the process is working. Where there is fruit, there is a root. The harvest has had abundant fruit since World War II. Hurt people hurt people. Wounded people wound people. If you feel that you can relate to the characteristics of an orphan heart, then healing ministry is something you might want to consider.

We have presented prayers and suggestions for healing the orphan heart. In no way is this a blueprint of techniques for healing. You may want to do this on your own. There are many books listed in the bibliography that you may read. However, there are significant advantages to having another person help you. Many healing prayer ministries are available for you, some of which are listed in this book.

Healing is a journey with the Father that has a beginning but continues a lifetime. Progress in this journey is a process in the Father's love. As long as you have progress, the process is working. However, there has to be a starting point. We can cause a paradigm shift in the emotional and spiritual culture of the world back towards the Father's love. Even if it is one person at a time.

ENDNOTES

Preface
1   Robert I Holmes, *Dealing With An Orphan Spirit*

Introduction
2   Stibbe, Mark, Father's Heart Leaders Conference 2009
3   http://www.cuttingedge.org/NEWS/n1017.html
4   http://en.wikipedia.org/wiki/1960s; http://answers.yahoo.com/ question/index?qid=20100409063344AAsftER
5   Rosemond, John. "All that self-esteem came at a cost," *Charlotte Observer–Carolina Living*, Tuesday, April 7, 2009
6   Ibid

War Children
7   Werner, Emmy E., *Through the Eyes of Innocents*, p211.
8   Ericsson, Kjersti, *Children of World War II*, p270-273
9   Ibid, p280

The Forgotten Fatherless
10   http://www.horsesofwisdom.com/orphan/kj_1.html, P.O. Box 607, Highland, NY 12528
11   Johnson ,Susan and Ann Bennett Mix, *Lost in the Victory*, p27-28
12   Ibid, p43
13   Ibid, p85
14   Ibid, p156
15   http://www.west.net/~awon/awbush.html
16   http://news.bbc.co.uk/2/hi/africa/3000990.stm
17   http://www.miramed.org/pdf/Nohappyend.pdf
18   *Nordic Journal of African Studies* 11(1): 93-113 (2002)
19   http://www.crossroads.org/pdf/Chosen_by_Grace_Overview .pps#4
20   *Nordic Journal of African Studies* 11(1): 93-113 (2002)
21   Hetland, Leif, School of Healing and Impartation 2008, Father Hunger

Chapter One
22   Frost, Jack. *Spiritual Slavery to Spiritual Sonship*, p63
23   Ibid, p64
24   http://www.gotquestions.org/tree knowledge good evil.html
25   http://www.gotquestions.org/tree knowledge good evil.html

26 James Jordan, FatherHeart Ministries, DVD "The Orphan Spirit"

27 James Jordan, FatherHeart Ministries, DVD "The Orphan Spirit"

28 James Jordan, FatherHeart Ministries, DVD "The Orphan Spirit"

29 James Jordan, FatherHeart Ministries, DVD "The Orphan Spirit"

30 http://images.acswebnetworks.com/1/401/Sermon62208office. pdf, (c) Judy Landt 2008, used by permission.

31 images.acswebnetworks.com, op.cit (c) Judy Landt 2008, used by permission.

32 Martin, Harold, Sermon July 2009, Lake Marion Christian Fellowship, Santee, SC.

33 http://nasb.scripturetext.com/luke/10.htm

34 Barkley,William. *The Gospel of Luke*, pp242-243

35 Frost, Jack, *Experiencing Fathers Embrace*, p 78

36 Ibid, p78

37 Ibid, p77

38 Ibid, p80

39 Winter, Jack, *The Home Coming*, p52

40 Winter, Jack, *The Home Coming*, p53

41 Ibid, p100

42 Winter, Jack, *The Home Coming*, p91

43 Ibid. p105

44 Shiloh Place Ministries. *Experiencing Father's Embrace* School

Chapter Two

45 Jordan, James. FatherHeart Ministries, DVD "The Orphan Spirit"

46 Mullen, Dr. Grant, M.D., *Why Do I Feel So Down When My Faith Should Lift Me Up?* p259

47 Frost, Jack, *Spiritual Slavery to Spiritual Sonship*, p37

48 Frost, Jack, *Spiritual Slavery to Spiritual Sonship*, p39

49 Frost, Jack, *Experiencing Father's Embrace*, p41

50 Martin, Harold, Lake Marion Christian Fellowship, Santee, SC.

51 Mullen, Dr. Grant, M.D., *Why Do I Feel So Down When My Faith Should Lift Me Up?* pp207-209

52 Frost, Jack, *Seeing The World Experience the Father's Healing Love*, Shiloh Place Ministries

53 http://bible.cc/ecclesiastes/4-10.htm

54 Judith, M. A., *Intimacy in Relationships*, Christian Healing Ministries, School of Healing Prayer, Level II, pp91-96

55 Mullen, Dr. Grant, M.D. *Why Do I Feel So Down When My Faith Should Lift Me Up?* p207-209

56 Frost, Jack, *Spiritual Slavery to Spiritual Sonship*, p43

57 Frost, Jack. *Experienceing Father's Embrace,* p81

58 Ibid, p100

59 Frost, Jack, *Would You Rather Be Right or Have a Relationship?* Part 1, Shiloh Place Ministries

60 Ibid

Chapter Three

61 Frost, Jack. *Spiritual Slavery to Spiritual Sonship*, p69

62 Ibid

63 Holmes, Robert I, "Dealing with An Orphan Spirit."

64 Kirschke, Rev. David, http://lifewaychurchnotes.blogspot.com/2007/02/exposing roots of spiritual orphans.html

65 Holmes, Robert, Article "Dealing with an Orphan Spirit," Storm Harvest Ministries, http://www.stormharvest.com.au

66 Frost, Jack, *From Slavery to Sonship* Part 1, Shiloh Place Ministries

67 Frost, Jack, *From Slavery to Sonship* Part 2, "How do you displace the orphan spirit?," Shiloh Place Ministries

Chapter Four

68 Kazenske, Donna J. Sure Word, Ministries, Litchfield, IL 62056

69 Frost, Jack, *Exposing the Roots of the Spiritual Orphan*, Shiloh Place Ministries

Chapter Five

70 Sanford, John and Paula. John Loren Sandford, *Restoring the Christian Family* (Lake Mary, FL: Charisma House, 2009), Used by permission, pp168-170

71 Frost, Jack, *Experiencing Father's Embrace*, p112

72 Linn, Dennis Sheila Linn, Matthew Linn, *Belonging: Bonds of Healing & Recovery*, pp 89-91

73 Baars, Conrad. *Born Only Once*, pp26-27

74 Linn, Sheila, Belonging, p91

75 Linn, Sheila, Belonging, p73

76 Ibid, p75

77 Ibid, p85

78 Ibid, p96

79 Linn, Dennis Sheila Linn, Matthew Linn, *Belonging: Bonds of Healing & Recovery*, pp94-95

80 Kazenske, Donna J, http://surewordministries.net/spiritualorphans.html, Spiritual Orphans Sure Word Ministries, Inc., Spiritual Orphans

Chapter Six

81 Mumford, Bob. *Agape Road*, pp 21

82 Mumford, Bob. *Agape Road*, pp 23

83 Mumford, Bob. *Agape Road*, pp 23-27

84 http://www.gotquestions.org/God different.html

85 http://forums.catholic.com/showthread.php?t=293607

86 Article "Why is the Old Testament God different than the New Testament God?, 15 August 2008, *The Virginian-Pilot*, http://hamptonroads.com/2008/08/old-testament-God-different-new-testament-God

87 Graham, Billy, Article "Is God in Old Testament Different from God in New?", *The Christian Post*, May 19, 2008 http://www.christianpost.com/Ministries

88 Paraphrased from *Healing Life's Hurts,* p66-67

89 Hetland, Leif, "Healing the Orphan Spirit" DVD, Global Mission Awareness, Killian, AL. 35645

90 Mullen, Dr. Grant, M.D. *Why do I feel so down when my faith should lift me up?* p 189

91 Paraphrased from *Healing Life's Hurts* p66-7

92 Shiloh Place Ministries. *Experiencing Father's Embrace* School

93 Shiloh Place Ministries. *Experiencing Father's Embrace* School

94 Frost, Jack, *Experiencing Father's Embrace,* p114

95 Frost, Jack, *Experiencing Father's Embrace,* p116

96 Frost, Jack, *Experiencing Father's Embrace,* p117

97 http://family.jrank.org/pages/1258/Parenting-Styles-Cultural-Differences-in-Guilt-Shame.html

98 Frost, Jack, *Experiencing Father's Embrace,* p117

99 Frost, Jack, *Experiencing Father's Embrace,* p118

100 Ibid

101 Ibid, p119

102 Ibid, p120

103 Martin, Harold. "Foundations Of The Father's Love" CD#4

104 Mumford, Bob, *Agape Road*, pp38

105 Mumford, Bob, *Agape Road*, pp38

106 Mumford, Bob, *Agape Road*, pp38-39

107 Mumford, Bob, *Agape Road*, pp39

108 Mumford, Bob, *Agape Road*, pp40

109 Shiloh Place Ministries. Experiencing Father's Embrace School

110 http://www.healthieryou.com/mhexpert/exp1082503b.html

111 Spitz, René A., and Cobliner, W. G. (1965). *The First Year of Life: A Psychoanalytic Study of Normal and Deviant Development of Object Relations.* New York: International Universities Press. 1965. 394 pp.

112 http://www.yfci.org/yfci/pdf/burundi.pdf

113 Ibid

114 Ibid

115 http://bible.cc/jeremiah/1-5.htm

116 http://bible.cc/acts/17-26.htm

Chapter Seven

117 Martin, Harold. "Foundations Of The Father's Love" CD#4

118 Stibbe, op. cit. p45

119 Frost, Jack, *Spiritual Slavery to Spiritual Sonship*, p189

120 http://www.pilgrimtours.com/church_history/italy/devotionals_history/Adoption.htm

121 Frost, Jack, *Spiritual Slavery to Spiritual Sonship*, p189

122 http://ejswensson.posterous.com/whos-your-daddy-check-out-this-inspiring-chri

123 Stibbe, Mark, From orphans to heirs, pp16

124 Stibbe, Mark, From orphans to heirs, pp16-17

125 Stibbe, op. cit. p32

126 Stibbe, op. cit. p54

127 http://nasb.scripturetext.com/ephesians/1.htm

128 Stibbe, op. cit. p92

129 Stibbe, op. cit. p102-103

130 Stibbe, op. cit. p109

131 Stibbe, op. cit. p110

132 Outler & Heitzenrater, John Wesley's Sermon's, p138

133 Stibbe, op. cit. p110-111

134 Stibbe, op. cit. p113

135 Stibbe, op. cit. p120-121

Healing the Orphan Heart

136 Mullen, Dr. Grant, M.D., *Why Do I Feel So Down When My Faith Should Lift Me Up?*

137 Hogue, Rodney, *Forgiveness*, copyright 2008, pp13-79 www.icgrace.org

138 Jordon, James, DVD "Heart of Sonship,"

139 Stibbe, op. cit. p94

140 Stibbe, op. cit. p94-95

141 Linn, Dennis and Matthew Linn, *Healing Life's Hurts*, pp28-29

142 Frost, Jack, *Exposing the Roots of the Spiritual Orphan*, Shiloh Place Ministries, Conway, SC.

Displacing the Orphan Heart

143 Shiloh Place Ministries, *Manual on Spiritual Fathering and Healthy Ministry*

144 Ibid

145 Adapted from material received from Bill and Deborah Fisher, P.O. Box 331031, Atlantic Beach, Florida 32233, (904) 249-3368, www.HotPursuitMinistries.com, www.FatherLovesJacksonville.com

146 Shiloh Place Ministries, Experiencing Father's Embrace School

147 Hetland, Leif, "Healing the Orphan Spirit" DVD, Global Mission Awareness, Killian, AL. 35645

Afterword

148 Emmy E. Werner, *Through The Eyes of Innocents*, (Westview Press, 2000) p177

Reviewers and Contributors

PASTOR HAROLD MARTIN
Santee, South Carolina

It took a supernatural encounter with God's love to transform my relationships. I entered into the Agape Reformation because after a few years in ministry I was struggling with self condemnation and anger and was well on my way to destroying those around me, as well as myself. I had started pastoring a church in Santee, South Carolina, in 1990. After only a few years in the ministry, I was a statistic – many of the bad things that you hear about pastors doing I was doing. The problem was my flesh; my soul realm was still out of control. Driven by religious striving, I ministered out of a need to be needed. I manipulated people and performed to get an unhealed need met. I had been raised in an alcoholic home with rejection and abandonment, and physical, verbal, and emotional abuse. I never knew how to get my need for love and acceptance met by my Heavenly Father, so I looked for love through ministry and in all the wrong places. I lived every day angry and did not know why. I didn't need a reason to be angry, only the opportunity to release that anger, and most of the time it was released against my family. Finally in February of 1998, I could not stand myself any longer. Even though I had forgiven my father for his abuse, Jack Frost led me through receiving forgiveness for my wrong responses to the wounding by my father: my rebellion against intimacy, chasing after counterfeit affections, and trying to fill a void in my heart with achievement and hyper religious activity. God's love began displacing the pain of the past and changed my life forever. It was not the end. I have not arrived, but it was the beginning of my process to wholeness and intimacy with Father God. I had been a man of faith, prayer, and the Word, but it took a supernatural encounter with God's love to transform my relationship with my wife and children and the motives behind the ministry. My approach to ministry is no longer authoritarian and to win approval, but now my passion is to simply be a demonstration of God's love to the next person I meet and I am enjoying the rest that I have found in this.

LEIF HETLAND
Global Mission Awareness Ministries

 Leif Hetland is from the small town Haugesund, in Norway. In 1984, after 5 years of rebellion, he heard the call of God to ministry. Through a glorious healing, deliverance and impartation of love, he ventured into the world of full time ministry. Leif Hetland is the founder of Global Mission Awareness based in Florence, Alabama. In 1995, while he was pastoring a small Baptist church in Norway, Leif was invited to a pastors' meeting where Randy Clark would lay hands on him and catapult his life and ministry into a whole new realm. Since that powerful experience, Leif has ministered in over 51 countries on 5 continents! He is one of the most influential Christian leaders in the Muslim nations today. His meetings and crusades are widely regarded for supernatural healings and signs and wonders.

www.GlobalMissionAwareness.com

REVEREND RUSS PARKER
Acorn Christian Healing Foundation

Russ Parker has been Director of Acorn Christian Healing Foundation in the United Kingdom since 1995, which exists to resource and educate the church in the Christian Healing Ministry. Part of Russ's contribution as Director has been to develop training materials. He is the author of a number of books, which include *Healing Dreams, Healing Death's Wounds, Free to Fail, Forgiveness is Healing,* and *Healing Wounded History* workbook. Russ travels extensively around the UK and abroad, lecturing and teaching in issues connected with the Christian healing and counseling ministry. Russ was a Baptist Pastor from 1972-77, ordained in the Church of England in 1981, Assistant Curate in Bolton 1981-1985, Incumbent of Christ Church, Coalville, 1985-1990, joined Acorn in 1990 and became its director in 1995. Russ was the co-founder and Director of Christian Care and Counsel, (now called The Haven) which is a Christian Counseling ministry based in the East Midlands, with over 25 volunteer and accredited counselors. He has a postgraduate degree in Dreams and Psychotherapy from Nottingham University. Russ was awarded a Doctor of Divinity from Columbia Evangelical Seminary in the United States in recognition of his outstanding contribution to Christian Ministry and his many writings and his teaching abilities. In particular, it was given for the standard of scholarship in his latest book, "Healing Wounded History," which is about reconciling people and healing places. Russ is married to Roz and lives near Farnham, Surrey. His hobbies are photography and visiting Celtic holy places. He supports the Liverpool Football Club, whether they are winning or losing!

PASTOR RODNEY HOGUE

 Pastor Rodney Hogue has been the senior pastor of Community of Grace since the summer of 1990. He has been active in the gospel ministry since the mid-1970s when he first got involved in youth and college ministries. He was the pastor of churches in Washington State for over eight years prior to coming to Community of Grace.

As evidenced in the programs offered in the church, Pastor Rodney is committed to the restoration of the saints into wholeness in Christ. His greatest joy is to see a destiny altered and a life changed by the power of God. Pastor Rodney, his wife Mary, and their three sons reside in nearby Castro Valley, California

Founders Jack and Trisha Frost

Shiloh Place was birthed in 1991 from Jack and Trisha's shared vision to create an environment where leaders could come and be safe. Later they formed a small group with three other couples where shared values would help bring healing to their lives and marriages. This group saw such change in their relationships and families that it overflowed to others, both leaders and churches. In 1996 Jack received a revelation of Father God's love that first impacted and transformed his family. As he began to share this testimony, and the lessons the family learned, Shiloh Place grew into a ministry of influence. Since that time individuals, families, churches, and leaders from all over the world have continued experiencing Father God's transforming love there. Even more, they are becoming influencers of change in their families, churches, and communities. God has added many to that small group and today the ministry team numbers more than 80 people.

www.ShilohPlace.org

Author
Bruce Brodowski

In 1995, after months of praying to God to use me in a healing prayer ministry, I awoke in the middle of the night to find my bedroom ceiling visibly gone. I was looking up into the sky of red, yellow, blue, green twinkling stars. I lifted my arm up towards the sky and said, "Father, what does all of this mean?" A bolt of light shot down onto my hand and the Father said, "I am calling you into a healing ministry." Now you would think I would have been amazed, elated, and overwhelmed by the experience. However, not believing what was happening, my answer was, "Lord, I would like a confirmation from three people who know nothing about what I have been praying for to come to me and tell me to let my hands be your hands."

Over the next several months I received confirmation from two people in off the wall messages. One was a lady who felt the Lord was telling her to read to me a scripture passage about being the healing hands of the Lord. One was in a prophecy given to me. However, the third confirmation came to me in an amazing way. I was attending a conference in Hickory, North Carolina, where the guest speakers were from the Pecos Monastery in New Mexico. Saturday night prayer teams prayed with people for their needs. After finishing on prayer team, I rushed over to receive prayer from two people who did not know me. We only had a couple of minutes before the closing ceremonies at eleven p.m. Prayer time with me was cut short because of this; however, Sister Geraldine from the Pecos Monastery said to me, "I don't know what this means, but the Lord wants me to tell you to let your hands be his hands." Thus began my journey into healing prayer ministry. Two years later, the Lord placed Ellen into my life, and confirmed to us that we were to marry each other.

We have served together heading the Intercession and Prayer Teams on Committees in both 1999 and 2004. We are graduates of the two- year lay ministry training of the Diocese of Charlotte. We also served on the Diocese of Charlotte Evangelization Committee and organized the first "Jam for Jesus" concert in Charlotte. We have been a part of Ecumenical Healing Ministries of Southwest Virginia since 2001, traveling to the Roanoke area to serve as prayer ministers at a Day of Healing Prayer. We are members of FCTH/USA (Fellowship of Christ the Healer/USA), an ecumenical gathering of clergy and lay people in various Christian healing ministries in the United States. We established Carolinas Ecumenical Healing Ministries (CEHM) in 2004. CEHM is a 501(c) (3) nonprofit organization registered in North Carolina. We are also members of Christ Mandate for Missions and the Apostolic Network of Global Awakening (ANGA). We have studied Spanish in Antigua, Guatemala and continue to improve our language skills in order to serve better on mission trips to South and Latin America. In March of 2008, we spent a week on a healing mission in Coban, Guatemala where healings were observed at San Marcos Catholic Church.

CEHM utilizes the training that has been developed by Christian Healing Ministries (CHM) in Jacksonville, Florida. www.christianhealingmin.org/about.htm We have received extensive training from CHM. Christian Healing Ministries "seeks to advance our Lord's ministry of healing through prayer." Christian Healing Ministries is dedicated to praying with those in need of healing in the physical, emotional, and spiritual areas of their lives and to teaching others about this often overlooked aspect of Christ's ministry. CEHM also utilizes training from other sources such as Elijah House, Reverend Russ Parker and Acorn Christian Foundation, the Healing Ministry of Fr. Leo Thomas O.P., SOZO, Embracing the Father's Love from Shiloh Place, and other sources in literature. Currently, we have completed training through Global Awakening School of Healing and Impartation and the ministry of Randy Clark. We are now registered members of the Apostolic Network of Global Awakening.

Through prayer, we bring people closer to Jesus Christ and his love. The healing prayer ministry of CEHM believes that Jesus heals mind, body, and soul through the ministry of prayer by His people. We minister to the spiritually wounded and broken people who have turned away from God and his love. We also pray for the physical healing of medical conditions. We have witnessed many healings through God's Grace.

Mission statement

We seek to lead people to a dynamic, intimate relationship with Jesus Christ and the Father through healing prayer. We seek to advance our Lord's ministry of healing of mind, body, and soul through prayer and our books. We are cross-denominational and are available to help churches and other organizations to established healing prayer programs. We seek to minister in other countries that invite us to teach, listen, and pray.

The Dad I Never Knew
by Bruce Brodowski

This book is carefully and articulately written. The reader shares along with the author his quest to know the man and to make sense of the life the son was destined to follow. Mr. Brodowski was definitely not alone in his experience but he has been most fortunate in finding a personal history upon which to draw. This reviewer hopes that some of those many others in Mr. Brodowski's situation will take heart and find some pride in those that gave so much for them.

This book is available through any bookseller and comes highly recommended by this reviewer as a part of history that should not be forgotten.

Reviewer: John Helman, M.A., Allbooks Reviews

Available

www.CEHM.info

Printed in Great Britain
by Amazon.co.uk, Ltd.,
Marston Gate.